# OpenCV with Python By Example

Build real-world computer vision applications and develop cool demos using OpenCV for Python

**Prateek Joshi**

**[PACKT]** open source✲
PUBLISHING    community experience distilled

BIRMINGHAM - MUMBAI

# OpenCV with Python By Example

First published: September 2015

Production reference: 1150915

Published by Packt Publishing Ltd.
Livery Place
35 Livery Street
Birmingham B3 2PB, UK.

ISBN 978-1-78528-393-2

www.packtpub.com

# Credits

**Author**
Prateek Joshi

**Reviewers**
Will Brennan

Gabriel Garrido Calvo

Pavan Kumar Pavagada Nagaraja

Marvin Smith

**Commissioning Editor**
Deepika Gaonkar

**Acquisition Editor**
Tushar Gupta

**Content Development Editor**
Sumeet Sawant

**Technical Editor**
Ryan Kochery

**Copy Editors**
Merilyn Pereira

Angad Singh

**Project Coordinator**
Shweta H Birwatkar

**Proofreader**
Safis Editing

**Indexer**
Tejal Daruwale Soni

**Graphics**
Jason Monteiro

**Production Coordinator**
Manu Joseph

**Cover Work**
Manu Joseph

# About the Author

**Prateek Joshi** is a computer vision researcher with a primary focus on content-based analysis. He is particularly interested in intelligent algorithms that can understand images to produce scene descriptions in terms of constituent objects. He has a master's degree from the University of Southern California, specializing in computer vision. He was elected to become a member of the Honor Society for academic excellence and an ambassador for the School of Engineering. Over the course of his career, he has worked for companies such as Nvidia, Microsoft Research, Qualcomm, and a couple of early stage start-ups in Silicon Valley.

His work in this field has resulted in multiple patents, tech demos, and research papers at major IEEE conferences. He has won many hackathons using a wide variety of technologies related to image recognition. He enjoys blogging about topics such as artificial intelligence, abstract mathematics, and cryptography. His blog has been visited by users in more than 200 countries, and he has been featured as a guest author in prominent tech magazines.

# About the Reviewers

**Will Brennan** is a software consultant based in London with experience in machine learning, image processing, and data mining. He is currently managing a start-up called SkyTales Ltd, which is a cloud-based 3D mapping and analytics service. SkyTales Ltd can work on a single video stream; the service is able to perform asset detection and tracking across large environments. You can also reach him on GitHub at `https://www.github.com/WillBrennan`.

**Gabriel Garrido Calvo** was born in 1986 in a small town called Burguillos del Cerro, located in Spain. In 2011, he was awarded a degree in software engineering by the University of Granada, Spain. He is passionate about programming languages and technologies.

Gabriel is currently working as a software engineer and team leader at trivago, which is one of the biggest hotel metasearch engines in the world, based in Düsseldorf, Germany.

**Pavan Kumar Pavagada Nagaraja** is currently working as a chief technology officer at Wearless Tech Inc., which is a start-up based in San Francisco, California. Here, Pavan is leading the development of "Cocoon Cam", which is a non-contact computer-vision-based camera system made to reliably monitor the heart rate, temperature, and breathing of infant patients. The product has received multiple awards, including the US National Science Foundation Innovation Corps award, Zahn Prize from The Moxie Foundation, and the Most Practical Solution award.

Pavan has a master's degree in computer science from the University of California, San Diego, and a bachelor's degree in electronics and communication from MSRIT, India. He has worked as a software programmer at the Apple headquarters in Cupertino, California, and as a technical marketing engineer at NetApp Inc., which is in Bangalore, India. He has technical experience in the fields of computer vision and machine learning, having published works in both of these areas.

**Marvin Smith** is currently a software engineer in the defense industry, specializing in photogrammetry and remote sensing. He received his BS degree in computer science from the University of Nevada, Reno, USA. His technical interests include high-performance computing, distributed image processing, and multispectral imagery exploitation. Prior to working in defense, Marvin held internships with the Intelligent Robotics Group at the NASA Ames Research Center and the Nevada Automotive Test Center.

# www.PacktPub.com

## Support files, eBooks, discount offers, and more

For support files and downloads related to your book, please visit www.PacktPub.com.

Did you know that Packt offers eBook versions of every book published, with PDF and ePub files available? You can upgrade to the eBook version at www.PacktPub. com and as a print book customer, you are entitled to a discount on the eBook copy. Get in touch with us at service@packtpub.com for more details.

At www.PacktPub.com, you can also read a collection of free technical articles, sign up for a range of free newsletters and receive exclusive discounts and offers on Packt books and eBooks.

https://www2.packtpub.com/books/subscription/packtlib

Do you need instant solutions to your IT questions? PacktLib is Packt's online digital book library. Here, you can search, access, and read Packt's entire library of books.

## Why subscribe?

- Fully searchable across every book published by Packt
- Copy and paste, print, and bookmark content
- On demand and accessible via a web browser

## Free access for Packt account holders

If you have an account with Packt at www.PacktPub.com, you can use this to access PacktLib today and view 9 entirely free books. Simply use your login credentials for immediate access.

# Table of Contents

# Preface

Computer vision is found everywhere in modern technology. OpenCV for Python enables us to run computer vision algorithms in real time. With the advent of powerful machines, we are getting more processing power to work with. Using this technology, we can seamlessly integrate our computer vision applications into the cloud. Web developers can develop complex applications without having to reinvent the wheel. This book is a practical tutorial that covers various examples at different levels, teaching you about the different functions of OpenCV and their actual implementations.

# What this book covers

*Chapter 1*, *Applying Geometric Transformations to Images*, explains how to apply geometric transformations to images. In this chapter, we will discuss affine and projective transformations, and see how we can use them to apply cool geometric effects to photos. The chapter will begin with the procedure to install OpenCV-Python on multiple platforms such as Mac OS X, Linux, and Windows. We will also learn how to manipulate an image in various ways, such as resizing, changing color spaces, and so on.

*Chapter 2*, *Detecting Edges and Applying Image Filters*, shows how to use fundamental image-processing operators and how we can use them to build bigger projects. We will discuss why we need edge detection and how it can be used in various different ways in computer vision applications. We will discuss image filtering and how we can use it to apply various visual effects to photos.

*Chapter 3, Cartoonizing an Image*, shows how to cartoonize a given image using image filters and other transformations. We will see how to use the webcam to capture a live video stream. We will discuss how to build a real-time application, where we extract information from each frame in the stream and display the result.

*Chapter 4, Detecting and Tracking Different Body Parts*, shows how to detect and track faces in a live video stream. We will discuss the face detection pipeline and see how we can use it to detect and track different body parts, such as eyes, ears, mouth, nose, and so on.

*Chapter 5, Extracting Features from an Image*, is about detecting the salient points (called keypoints) in an image. We will discuss why these salient points are important and how we can use them to understand the image content. We will talk about the different techniques that can be used to detect salient points and extract features from an image.

*Chapter 6, Creating a Panoramic Image*, shows how to create a panoramic image by stitching multiple images of the same scene together.

*Chapter 7, Seam Carving*, shows how to do content-aware image resizing. We will discuss how to detect "interesting" parts in an image and see how we can resize a given image without deteriorating those interesting parts.

*Chapter 8, Detecting Shapes and Segmenting an Image*, shows how to perform image segmentation. We will discuss how to partition a given image into its constituent parts in the best possible way. You will also learn how to separate the foreground from the background in an image.

*Chapter 9, Object Tracking*, shows you how to track different objects in a live video stream. At the end of this chapter, you will be able to track any object in a live video stream that is captured through the webcam.

*Chapter 10, Object Recognition*, shows how to build an object recognition system. We will discuss how to use this knowledge to build a visual search engine.

*Chapter 11, Stereo Vision and 3D Reconstruction*, shows how to reconstruct the depth map using stereo images. You will learn how to achieve a 3D reconstruction of a scene from a set of images.

*Chapter 12, Augmented Reality*, shows how to build an augmented reality application. By the end of this chapter, you will be able to build a fun augmented reality project using the webcam.

# What you need for this book

You'll need the following software:

- OpenCV 2.4.9
- numpy 1.9.2
- scipy 0.15.1
- scikit-learn 0.16.1

The hardware specifications requirement is any computer with at least 4GB DDR3 RAM.

# Who this book is for

This book is intended for Python developers who are new to OpenCV and want to develop computer vision applications with OpenCV-Python. This book is also useful for generic software developers who want to deploy computer vision applications on the cloud. It would be helpful to have some familiarity with basic mathematical concepts, such as vectors, matrices, and so on.

# Conventions

In this book, you will find a number of text styles that distinguish between different kinds of information. Here are some examples of these styles and an explanation of their meaning.

Code words in text, database table names, folder names, filenames, file extensions, pathnames, dummy URLs, user input, and Twitter handles are shown as follows: "We use a function called getPerspectiveTransform to get the transformation matrix."

A block of code is set as follows:

```
cv2.imshow('Input', img)
cv2.imshow('Output', img_output)
cv2.waitKey()
```

Any command-line input or output is written as follows:

```
$ make -j4
$ sudo make install
```

**New terms** and **important words** are shown in bold. Words that you see on the screen, for example, in menus or dialog boxes, appear in the text like this: "The **tx** and **ty** values are the X and Y translation values."

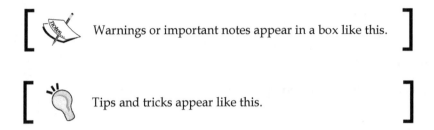

Warnings or important notes appear in a box like this.

Tips and tricks appear like this.

# Reader feedback

Feedback from our readers is always welcome. Let us know what you think about this book—what you liked or disliked. Reader feedback is important for us as it helps us develop titles that you will really get the most out of.

To send us general feedback, simply e-mail feedback@packtpub.com, and mention the book's title in the subject of your message.

If there is a topic that you have expertise in and you are interested in either writing or contributing to a book, see our author guide at www.packtpub.com/authors.

# Customer support

Now that you are the proud owner of a Packt book, we have a number of things to help you to get the most from your purchase.

## Downloading the example code

You can download the example code files from your account at http://www.packtpub.com for all the Packt Publishing books you have purchased. If you purchased this book elsewhere, you can visit http://www.packtpub.com/support and register to have the files e-mailed directly to you.

# Downloading the color images of this book

We also provide you with a PDF file that has color images of the screenshots/ diagrams used in this book. The color images will help you better understand the changes in the output. You can download this file from `https://www.packtpub. com/sites/default/files/downloads/B04554_Graphics.pdf`.

# Errata

Although we have taken every care to ensure the accuracy of our content, mistakes do happen. If you find a mistake in one of our books—maybe a mistake in the text or the code—we would be grateful if you could report this to us. By doing so, you can save other readers from frustration and help us improve subsequent versions of this book. If you find any errata, please report them by visiting `http://www.packtpub. com/submit-errata`, selecting your book, clicking on the **Errata Submission Form** link, and entering the details of your errata. Once your errata are verified, your submission will be accepted and the errata will be uploaded to our website or added to any list of existing errata under the Errata section of that title.

To view the previously submitted errata, go to `https://www.packtpub.com/books/ content/support` and enter the name of the book in the search field. The required information will appear under the **Errata** section.

# Piracy

Piracy of copyrighted material on the Internet is an ongoing problem across all media. At Packt, we take the protection of our copyright and licenses very seriously. If you come across any illegal copies of our works in any form on the Internet, please provide us with the location address or website name immediately so that we can pursue a remedy.

Please contact us at `copyright@packtpub.com` with a link to the suspected pirated material.

We appreciate your help in protecting our authors and our ability to bring you valuable content.

# Questions

If you have a problem with any aspect of this book, you can contact us at `questions@packtpub.com`, and we will do our best to address the problem.

# 1
# Applying Geometric Transformations to Images

In this chapter, we are going to learn how to apply cool geometric effects to images. Before we get started, we need to install OpenCV-Python. We will discuss how to install the necessary tools and packages as well.

By the end of this chapter, you will know:

- How to install OpenCV-Python
- How to read, display, and save images
- How to convert between multiple color spaces
- How to apply geometric transformations like translation, rotation, and scaling
- How to use affine and projective transformations to apply funny geometric effects on photos

## Installing OpenCV-Python

Let's see how to install OpenCV with Python support on multiple platforms.

## Windows

In order to get OpenCV-Python up and running, we need to perform the following steps:

1. Install Python: Make sure you have Python 2.7.x installed on your machine. If you don't have it, you can install it from `https://www.python.org/downloads/windows/`

2.  Install NumPy: NumPy is a great package to do numerical computing in Python. It is very powerful and has a wide variety of functions. OpenCV-Python plays nicely with NumPy, and we will be using this package a lot, during the course of this book. You can install the latest version from `http://sourceforge.net/projects/numpy/files/NumPy/`

We need to install all these packages in their default locations. Once we install Python and NumPy, we need to ensure that they're working fine. Open up the Python shell and type the following:

```
>>> import numpy
```

If the installation has gone well, this shouldn't throw any error. Once you confirm it, you can go ahead and download the latest OpenCV version from `http://opencv.org/downloads.html`

Once you finish downloading it, double-click to install it. We need to make a couple of changes, as follows:

1.  Navigate to `opencv/build/python/2.7/`
2.  You will see a file named `cv2.pyd`. Copy this file to `C:/Python27/lib/site-packages`

You're all set! Let's make sure that OpenCV is working. Open up the Python shell and type the following:

```
>>> import cv2
```

If you don't see any errors, then you are good to go! You are now ready to use OpenCV-Python.

# Mac OS X

To install OpenCV-Python, we will be using **Homebrew**. Homebrew is a great package manager for Mac OS X and it will come in handy when you are installing various libraries and utilities on OS X. If you don't have Homebrew, you can install it by running the following command on your terminal:

```
$ ruby -e "$(curl -fsSL
https://raw.githubusercontent.com/Homebrew/install/master/install)"
```

Even though OS X comes with inbuilt Python, we need to install Python using Homebrew to make our lives easier. This version is called brewed Python. Once you install Homebrew, the next step is to install brewed Python. Open up the terminal and type the following:

```
$ brew install python
```

This will automatically install `pip` as well. Pip is a package management tool to install packages in Python and we will be using it to install other packages. Let's make sure the brewed Python is working correctly. Go to your terminal and type the following:

```
$ which python
```

You should see `/usr/local/bin/python` printed on the terminal. This means that we are using the brewed Python and not the inbuilt system Python. Now that we have installed brewed Python, we can go ahead and add the repository, `homebrew/science`, which is where OpenCV is located. Open the terminal and run the following command:

```
$ brew tap homebrew/science
```

Make sure the package NumPy is installed. If not, run the following in your terminal:

```
$ pip install numpy
```

Now, we are ready to install OpenCV. Go ahead and run the following command from your terminal:

```
$ brew install opencv --with-tbb --with-opengl
```

OpenCV is now installed on your machine and you can find it at `/usr/local/Cellar/opencv/2.4.9/`. You can't use it just yet. We need to tell Python where to find our OpenCV packages. Let's go ahead and do that by symlinking the OpenCV files. Run the following commands from your terminal:

```
$ cd /Library/Python/2.7/site-packages/
$ ln -s /usr/local/Cellar/opencv/2.4.9/lib/python2.7/site-packages/cv.py
cv.py
$ ln -s /usr/local/Cellar/opencv/2.4.9/lib/python2.7/site-packages/cv2.so
cv2.so
```

You're all set! Let's see if it's installed properly. Open up the Python shell and type the following:

```
>>> import cv2
```

If the installation went well, you will not see any error message. You are now ready to use OpenCV in Python.

# Linux (for Ubuntu)

Before we start, we need to install some dependencies. Let's install them using the package manager as shown below:

```
$ sudo apt-get -y install libopencv-dev build-essential cmake
libdc1394-22 libdc1394-22-dev libjpeg-dev libpng12-dev
libtiff4-dev libjasper-dev libavcodec-dev libavformat-dev
libswscale-dev libxine-dev libgstreamer0.10-dev
libgstreamer-plugins-base0.10-dev libv4l-dev libtbb-dev libqt4-dev
libmp3lame-dev libopencore-amrnb-dev libopencore-amrwb-dev
libtheora-dev libvorbis-dev libxvidcore-dev x264 v4l-utils
python-scipy python-pip python-virtualenv
```

Now that you have installed the necessary packages, let's go ahead and build OpenCV with Python support:

```
$ wget "https://github.com/Itseez/opencv/archive/2.4.9.tar.gz" -O
./opencv/opencv.tar.gz
```

```
$ cd opencv
```

```
$ tar xvzf opencv.tar.gz -C .
```

```
$ mkdir release
```

```
$ cd release
```

```
$ sudo apt-get -y install cmake
```

```
$ cmake -D CMAKE_BUILD_TYPE=RELEASE -D
CMAKE_INSTALL_PREFIX=/usr/local -D BUILD_PYTHON_SUPPORT=ON -D
WITH_XINE=ON -D WITH_OPENGL=ON -D WITH_TBB=ON -D WITH_EIGEN=ON -D
BUILD_EXAMPLES=ON -D BUILD_NEW_PYTHON_SUPPORT=ON -D WITH_V4L=ON
../
```

```
$ make -j4
```

```
$ sudo make install
```

Let's make sure that it's installed correctly. Open up the Python shell and type the following:

```
>>> import cv2
```

If you don't see any errors, you are good to go.

If you have any other Linux distribution, please refer to the OpenCV downloads page (http://opencv.org/downloads.html) for installation details.

# Reading, displaying, and saving images

Let's see how we can load an image in OpenCV-Python. Create a file named first_program.py and open it in your favorite code editor. Create a folder named images in the current folder and make sure that you have an image named input.jpg in that folder.

Once you do that, add the following lines to that Python file:

```
import cv2
img = cv2.imread('./images/input.jpg')
cv2.imshow('Input image', img)
cv2.waitKey()
```

If you run the preceding program, you will see an image being displayed in a new window.

# What just happened?

Let's understand the previous piece of code, line by line. In the first line, we are importing the OpenCV library. We need this for all the functions we will be using in the code. In the second line, we are reading the image and storing it in a variable. OpenCV uses NumPy data structures to store the images. You can learn more about NumPy at http://www.numpy.org

So if you open up the Python shell and type the following, you will see the datatype printed on the terminal:

```
>>> import cv2
>>> img = cv2.imread('./images/input.jpg')
>>> type(img)
<type 'numpy.ndarray'>
```

In the next line, we display the image in a new window. The first argument in cv2.imshow is the name of the window. The second argument is the image you want to display.

You must be wondering why we have the last line here. The function, cv2.waitKey(), is used in OpenCV for keyboard binding. It takes a number as an argument, and that number indicates the time in milliseconds. Basically, we use this function to wait for a specified duration, until we encounter a keyboard event. The program stops at this point, and waits for you to press any key to continue. If we don't pass any argument or if we pass 0 as the argument, this function will wait for a keyboard event indefinitely.

# Loading and saving an image

OpenCV provides multiple ways of loading an image. Let's say we want to load a color image in grayscale mode. We can do that using the following piece of code:

```
import cv2
gray_img = cv2.imread('images/input.jpg', cv2.IMREAD_GRAYSCALE)
cv2.imshow('Grayscale', gray_img)
cv2.waitKey()
```

Here, we are using the flag cv2.IMREAD_GRAYSCALE to load the image in grayscale mode. You can see that from the image being displayed in the new window. Next, is the input image:

Following is the corresponding grayscale image:

We can save this image into a file as well:

```
cv2.imwrite('images/output.jpg', gray_img)
```

This will save the grayscale image into an output file named output.jpg. Make sure you get comfortable with reading, displaying, and saving images in OpenCV, because we will be doing this quite a bit during the course of this book.

# Image color spaces

In computer vision and image processing, color space refers to a specific way of organizing colors. A color space is actually a combination of two things: a color model and a mapping function. The reason we want color models is because it helps us in representing pixel values using tuples. The mapping function maps the color model to the set of all possible colors that can be represented.

There are many different color spaces that are useful. Some of the more popular color spaces are RGB, YUV, HSV, Lab, and so on. Different color spaces provide different advantages. We just need to pick the color space that's right for the given problem. Let's take a couple of color spaces and see what information they provide:

- **RGB**: It's probably the most popular color space. It stands for Red, Green, and Blue. In this color space, each color is represented as a weighted combination of red, green, and blue. So every pixel value is represented as a tuple of three numbers corresponding to red, green, and blue. Each value ranges between 0 and 255.

- **YUV**: Even though RGB is good for many purposes, it tends to be very limited for many real life applications. People started thinking about different methods to separate the intensity information from the color information. Hence, they came up with the YUV color space. Y refers to the luminance or intensity, and U/V channels represent color information. This works well in many applications because the human visual system perceives intensity information very differently from color information.

- **HSV**: As it turned out, even YUV was still not good enough for some of the applications. So people started thinking about how humans perceive color and they came up with the HSV color space. HSV stands for Hue, Saturation, and Value. This is a cylindrical system where we separate three of the most primary properties of colors and represent them using different channels. This is closely related to how the human visual system understands color. This gives us a lot of flexibility as to how we can handle images.

# Converting between color spaces

Considering all the color spaces, there are around 190 conversion options available in OpenCV. If you want to see a list of all available flags, go to the Python shell and type the following:

```
>>> import cv2
>>> print [x for x in dir(cv2) if x.startswith('COLOR_')]
```

You will see a list of options available in OpenCV for converting from one color space to another. We can pretty much convert any color space into any other color space. Let's see how we can convert a color image into a grayscale image:

```
import cv2
img = cv2.imread('./images/input.jpg')
gray_img = cv2.cvtColor(img, cv2.COLOR_BGR2GRAY)
cv2.imshow('Grayscale image', gray_img)
cv2.waitKey()
```

# What just happened?

We use the function `cvtColor` to convert between color spaces. The first argument is the input image and the second argument specifies the color space conversion. You can convert to YUV by using the following flag:

```
yuv_img = cv2.cvtColor(img, cv2.COLOR_BGR2YUV)
```

The image will look something like the following one:

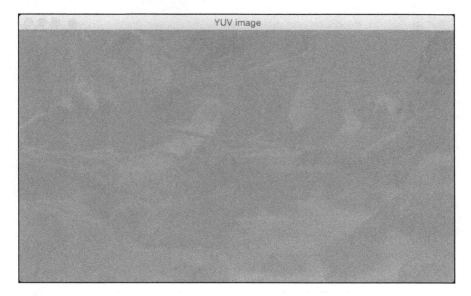

This may look like a deteriorated version of the original image, but it's not. Let's separate out the three channels:

```
cv2.imshow('Y channel', yuv_img[:, :, 0])
cv2.imshow('U channel', yuv_img[:, :, 1])
cv2.imshow('V channel', yuv_img[:, :, 2])
cv2.waitKey()
```

Since `yuv_img` is a numPy array, we can separate out the three channels by slicing it. If you look at `yuv_img.shape`, you will see that it is a 3D array whose dimensions are `NUM_ROWS x NUM_COLUMNS x NUM_CHANNELS`. So once you run the preceding piece of code, you will see three different images. Following is the Y channel:

The Y channel is basically the grayscale image. Next is the U channel:

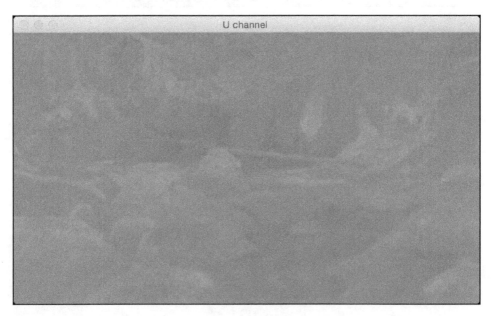

And lastly, the v channel:

As we can see here, the Y channel is the same as the grayscale image. It represents the intensity values. The U and V channels represent the color information.

Let's convert to HSV and see what happens:

```
hsv_img = cv2.cvtColor(img, cv2.COLOR_BGR2HSV)
cv2.imshow('HSV image', hsv_img)
```

Again, let's separate the channels:

```
cv2.imshow('H channel', hsv_img[:, :, 0])
cv2.imshow('S channel', hsv_img[:, :, 1])
cv2.imshow('V channel', hsv_img[:, :, 2])
cv2.waitKey()
```

If you run the preceding piece of code, you will see three different images. Take a look at the H channel:

Next is the S channel:

Following is the v channel:

This should give you a basic idea of how to convert between color spaces. You can play around with more color spaces to see what the images look like. We will discuss the relevant color spaces as and when we encounter them during subsequent chapters.

# Image translation

In this section, we will discuss about shifting an image. Let's say we want to move the image within our frame of reference. In computer vision terminology, this is referred to as translation. Let's go ahead and see how we can do that:

```
import cv2
import numpy as np

img = cv2.imread('images/input.jpg')
num_rows, num_cols = img.shape[:2]

translation_matrix = np.float32([ [1,0,70], [0,1,110] ])
img_translation = cv2.warpAffine(img, translation_matrix, (num_cols,
num_rows))
cv2.imshow('Translation', img_translation)
cv2.waitKey()
```

If you run the preceding code, you will see something like the following:

# What just happened?

To understand the preceding code, we need to understand how warping works. Translation basically means that we are shifting the image by adding/subtracting the X and Y coordinates. In order to do this, we need to create a transformation matrix, as shown as follows:

$$T = \begin{bmatrix} 1 & 0 & t_x \\ 0 & 1 & t_y \end{bmatrix}$$

Here, the **tx** and **ty** values are the X and Y translation values, that is, the image will be moved by X units towards the right, and by Y units downwards. So once we create a matrix like this, we can use the function, warpAffine, to apply to our image. The third argument in warpAffine refers to the number of rows and columns in the resulting image. Since the number of rows and columns is the same as the original image, the resultant image is going to get cropped. The reason for this is because we didn't have enough space in the output when we applied the translation matrix. To avoid cropping, we can do something like this:

```
img_translation = cv2.warpAffine(img, translation_matrix,
(num_cols + 70, num_rows + 110))
```

If you replace the corresponding line in our program with the preceding line, you will see the following image:

Let's say you want to move the image in the middle of a bigger image frame; we can do something like this by carrying out the following:

```
import cv2
import numpy as np

img = cv2.imread('images/input.jpg')
num_rows, num_cols = img.shape[:2]

translation_matrix = np.float32([ [1,0,70], [0,1,110] ])
img_translation = cv2.warpAffine(img, translation_matrix, (num_cols +
70, num_rows + 110))
translation_matrix = np.float32([ [1,0,-30], [0,1,-50] ])
img_translation = cv2.warpAffine(img_translation, translation_matrix,
(num_cols + 70 + 30, num_rows + 110 + 50))
cv2.imshow('Translation', img_translation)
cv2.waitKey()
```

If you run the preceding code, you will see an image like the following:

# Image rotation

In this section, we will see how to rotate a given image by a certain angle. We can do it using the following piece of code:

```
import cv2
import numpy as np

img = cv2.imread('images/input.jpg')
num_rows, num_cols = img.shape[:2]

rotation_matrix = cv2.getRotationMatrix2D((num_cols/2, num_rows/2),
30, 1)
img_rotation = cv2.warpAffine(img, rotation_matrix, (num_cols, num_
rows))
cv2.imshow('Rotation', img_rotation)
cv2.waitKey()
```

If you run the preceding code, you will see an image like this:

# What just happened?

In order to understand this, let's see how we handle rotation mathematically. Rotation is also a form of transformation, and we can achieve it by using the following transformation matrix:

$$R = \begin{bmatrix} \cos\theta & -\sin\theta \\ \sin\theta & \cos\theta \end{bmatrix}$$

Here, $\theta$ is the angle of rotation in the counterclockwise direction. OpenCV provides closer control over the creation of this matrix through the function, `getRotationMatrix2D`. We can specify the point around which the image would be rotated, the angle of rotation in degrees, and a scaling factor for the image. Once we have the transformation matrix, we can use the `warpAffine` function to apply this matrix to any image.

As we can see from the previous figure, the image content goes out of boundary and gets cropped. In order to prevent this, we need to provide enough space in the output image. Let's go ahead and do that using the translation functionality we discussed earlier:

```
import cv2
import numpy as np

img = cv2.imread('images/input.jpg')
num_rows, num_cols = img.shape[:2]

translation_matrix = np.float32([ [1,0,int(0.5*num_cols)],
[0,1,int(0.5*num_rows)] ])
2*num_cols, 2*num_rows))
rotation_matrix = cv2.getRotationMatrix2D((num_cols, num_rows), 30,
img_translation = cv2.warpAffine(img, translation_matrix, (1)
img_rotation = cv2.warpAffine(img_translation, rotation_matrix,
(2*num_cols, 2*num_rows))

cv2.imshow('Rotation', img_rotation)
cv2.waitKey()
```

If we run the preceding code, we will see something like this:

# Image scaling

In this section, we will discuss about resizing an image. This is one of the most common operations in computer vision. We can resize an image using a `scaling` factor, or we can resize it to a particular size. Let's see how to do that:

```
img_scaled = cv2.resize(img,None,fx=1.2, fy=1.2, interpolation =
cv2.INTER_LINEAR)
cv2.imshow('Scaling - Linear Interpolation', img_scaled)
img_scaled = cv2.resize(img,None,fx=1.2, fy=1.2, interpolation =
cv2.INTER_CUBIC)
cv2.imshow('Scaling - Cubic Interpolation', img_scaled)
img_scaled = cv2.resize(img,(450, 400), interpolation = cv2.INTER_
AREA)
cv2.imshow('Scaling - Skewed Size', img_scaled)
cv2.waitKey()
```

# What just happened?

Whenever we resize an image, there are multiple ways to fill in the pixel values. When we are enlarging an image, we need to fill up the pixel values in between pixel locations. When we are shrinking an image, we need to take the best representative value. When we are scaling by a non-integer value, we need to interpolate values appropriately, so that the quality of the image is maintained. There are multiple ways to do interpolation. If we are enlarging an image, it's preferable to use linear or cubic interpolation. If we are shrinking an image, it's preferable to use the area-based interpolation. Cubic interpolation is computationally more complex, and hence slower than linear interpolation. But the quality of the resulting image will be higher.

OpenCV provides a function called `resize` to achieve image scaling. If you don't specify a size (by using `None`), then it expects the X and Y scaling factors. In our example, the image will be enlarged by a factor of 1.2. If we do the same enlargement using cubic interpolation, we can see that the quality improves, as seen in the following figure. The following screenshot shows what linear interpolation looks like:

Here is the corresponding cubic interpolation:

If we want to resize it to a particular size, we can use the format shown in the last resize instance. We can basically skew the image and resize it to whatever size we want. The output will look something like the following:

# Affine transformations

In this section, we will discuss about the various generalized geometrical transformations of 2D images. We have been using the function warpAffine quite a bit over the last couple of sections, it's about time we understood what's happening underneath.

Before talking about affine transformations, let's see what Euclidean transformations are. Euclidean transformations are a type of geometric transformations that preserve length and angle measure. As in, if we take a geometric shape and apply Euclidean transformation to it, the shape will remain unchanged. It might look rotated, shifted, and so on, but the basic structure will not change. So technically, lines will remain lines, planes will remain planes, squares will remain squares, and circles will remain circles.

Coming back to affine transformations, we can say that they are generalizations of Euclidean transformations. Under the realm of affine transformations, lines will remain lines but squares might become rectangles or parallelograms. Basically, affine transformations don't preserve lengths and angles.

In order to build a general affine transformation matrix, we need to define the control points. Once we have these control points, we need to decide where we want them to be mapped. In this particular situation, all we need are three points in the source image, and three points in the output image. Let's see how we can convert an image into a parallelogram-like image:

```
import cv2
import numpy as np

img = cv2.imread('images/input.jpg')
rows, cols = img.shape[:2]

src_points = np.float32([[0,0], [cols-1,0], [0,rows-1]])
dst_points = np.float32([[0,0], [int(0.6*(cols-1)),0], [int(0.4*(cols-1)),rows-1]])
affine_matrix = cv2.getAffineTransform(src_points, dst_points)
img_output = cv2.warpAffine(img, affine_matrix, (cols,rows))

cv2.imshow('Input', img)
cv2.imshow('Output', img_output)
cv2.waitKey()
```

# What just happened?

As we discussed earlier, we are defining control points. We just need three points to get the affine transformation matrix. We want the three points in `src_points` to be mapped to the corresponding points in `dst_points`. We are mapping the points as shown in the following:

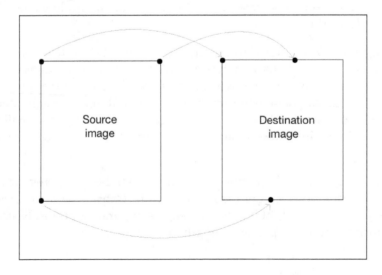

To get the transformation matrix, we have a function called `getAffineTransform` in OpenCV. Once we have the affine transformation matrix, we use the `warpAffine` function to apply this matrix to the input image.

Following is the input image:

If you run the preceding code, the output will look something like this:

We can also get the mirror image of the input image. We just need to change the control points in the following way:

```
src_points = np.float32([[0,0], [cols-1,0], [0,rows-1]])
dst_points = np.float32([[cols-1,0], [0,0], [cols-1,rows-1]])
```

Here, the mapping looks something like this:

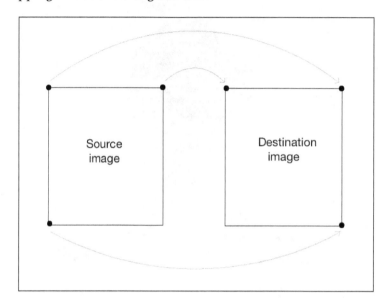

If you replace the corresponding lines in our affine transformation code with these two lines, you will get the following result:

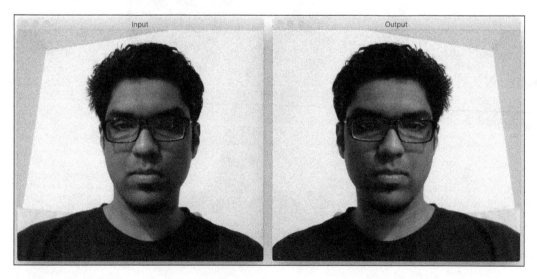

# Projective transformations

Affine transformations are nice, but they impose certain restrictions. A projective transformation, on the other hand, gives us more freedom. It is also referred to as **homography**. In order to understand projective transformations, we need to understand how projective geometry works. We basically describe what happens to an image when the point of view is changed. For example, if you are standing right in front of a sheet of paper with a square drawn on it, it will look like a square. Now, if you start tilting that sheet of paper, the square will start looking more and more like a trapezoid. Projective transformations allow us to capture this dynamic in a nice mathematical way. These transformations preserve neither sizes nor angles, but they do preserve incidence and cross-ratio.

> You can read more about incidence and cross-ratio at http://en.wikipedia.org/wiki/Incidence_(geometry) and http://en.wikipedia.org/wiki/Cross-ratio.

Now that we know what projective transformations are, let's see if we can extract more information here. We can say that any two images on a given plane are related by a homography. As long as they are in the same plane, we can transform anything into anything else. This has many practical applications such as augmented reality, image rectification, image registration, or the computation of camera motion between two images. Once the camera rotation and translation have been extracted from an estimated homography matrix, this information may be used for navigation, or to insert models of 3D objects into an image or video. This way, they are rendered with the correct perspective and it will look like they were part of the original scene.

Let's go ahead and see how to do this:

```
import cv2
import numpy as np

img = cv2.imread('images/input.jpg')
rows, cols = img.shape[:2]

src_points = np.float32([[0,0], [cols-1,0], [0,rows-1], [cols-1,rows-1]])
dst_points = np.float32([[0,0], [cols-1,0], [int(0.33*cols),rows-1], [int(0.66*cols),rows-1]])
projective_matrix = cv2.getPerspectiveTransform(src_points, dst_points)
img_output = cv2.warpPerspective(img, projective_matrix, (cols,rows))

cv2.imshow('Input', img)
cv2.imshow('Output', img_output)
cv2.waitKey()
```

If you run the preceding code, you will see a funny looking output like the following screenshot:

# What just happened?

We can choose four control points in the source image and map them to the destination image. Parallel lines will not remain parallel lines after the transformation. We use a function called getPerspectiveTransform to get the transformation matrix.

Let's apply a couple of fun effects using projective transformation and see what they look like. All we need to do is change the control points to get different effects.

Here's an example:

The control points are as shown next:

```
src_points = np.float32([[0,0], [0,rows-1], [cols/2,0],
[cols/2,rows-1]])
dst_points = np.float32([[0,100], [0,rows-101], [cols/2,0],
[cols/2,rows-1]])
```

As an exercise, you should map the above points on a plane and see how the points are mapped (just like we did earlier, while discussing Affine Transformations). You will get a good understanding about the mapping system, and you can create your own control points.

# Image warping

Let's have some more fun with the images and see what else we can achieve. Projective transformations are pretty flexible, but they still impose some restrictions on how we can transform the points. What if we want to do something completely random? We need more control, right? As it so happens, we can do that as well. We just need to create our own mapping, and it's not that difficult. Following are a few effects you can achieve with image warping:

Here is the code to create these effects:

```python
import cv2
import numpy as np
import math

img = cv2.imread('images/input.jpg', cv2.IMREAD_GRAYSCALE)
rows, cols = img.shape

#####################
# Vertical wave

img_output = np.zeros(img.shape, dtype=img.dtype)

for i in range(rows):
    for j in range(cols):
        offset_x = int(25.0 * math.sin(2 * 3.14 * i / 180))
        offset_y = 0
        if j+offset_x < rows:
            img_output[i,j] = img[i,(j+offset_x)%cols]
        else:
            img_output[i,j] = 0

cv2.imshow('Input', img)
cv2.imshow('Vertical wave', img_output)

#####################
# Horizontal wave

img_output = np.zeros(img.shape, dtype=img.dtype)

for i in range(rows):
    for j in range(cols):
        offset_x = 0
        offset_y = int(16.0 * math.sin(2 * 3.14 * j / 150))
        if i+offset_y < rows:
            img_output[i,j] = img[(i+offset_y)%rows,j]
        else:
            img_output[i,j] = 0

cv2.imshow('Horizontal wave', img_output)

#####################
```

```
# Both horizontal and vertical

img_output = np.zeros(img.shape, dtype=img.dtype)

for i in range(rows):
    for j in range(cols):
        offset_x = int(20.0 * math.sin(2 * 3.14 * i / 150))
        offset_y = int(20.0 * math.cos(2 * 3.14 * j / 150))
        if i+offset_y < rows and j+offset_x < cols:
            img_output[i,j] = img[(i+offset_y)%rows, (j+offset_x)%cols]
        else:
            img_output[i,j] = 0

cv2.imshow('Multidirectional wave', img_output)

#####################
# Concave effect

img_output = np.zeros(img.shape, dtype=img.dtype)

for i in range(rows):
    for j in range(cols):
        offset_x = int(128.0 * math.sin(2 * 3.14 * i / (2*cols)))
        offset_y = 0
        if j+offset_x < cols:
            img_output[i,j] = img[i, (j+offset_x)%cols]
        else:
            img_output[i,j] = 0

cv2.imshow('Concave', img_output)

cv2.waitKey()
```

# Summary

In this chapter, we learned how to install OpenCV-Python on various platforms. We discussed how to read, display, and save images. We talked about the importance of various color spaces and how we can convert between multiple color spaces. We learned how to apply geometric transformations to images and understood how to use those transformations to achieve cool geometric effects. We discussed the underlying formulation of transformation matrices and how we can formulate different kinds of transformations based on our needs. We learned how to select control points based on the required geometric transformation. We discussed about projective transformations and learned how to use image warping to achieve any given geometric effect. In the next chapter, we are going to discuss edge detection and image filtering. We can apply a lot of visual effects using image filters, and the underlying formation gives us a lot of freedom to manipulate images in creative ways.

# 2
# Detecting Edges and Applying Image Filters

In this chapter, we are going to see how to apply cool visual effects to images. We will learn how to use fundamental image processing operators. We are going to discuss edge detection and how we can use image filters to apply various effects on photos.

By the end of this chapter, you will know:

- What is 2D convolution and how to use it
- How to blur an image
- How to detect edges in an image
- How to apply motion blur to an image
- How to sharpen and emboss an image
- How to erode and dilate an image
- How to create a vignette filter
- How to enhance image contrast

**Downloading the example code**

You can download the example code files from your account at http://www.packtpub.com for all the Packt Publishing books you have purchased. If you purchased this book elsewhere, you can visit http://www.packtpub.com/support and register to have the files e-mailed directly to you.

# 2D convolution

Convolution is a fundamental operation in image processing. We basically apply a mathematical operator to each pixel and change its value in some way. To apply this mathematical operator, we use another matrix called a **kernel**. The kernel is usually much smaller in size than the input image. For each pixel in the image, we take the kernel and place it on top such that the center of the kernel coincides with the pixel under consideration. We then multiply each value in the kernel matrix with the corresponding values in the image, and then sum it up. This is the new value that will be substituted in this position in the output image.

Here, the kernel is called the "image filter" and the process of applying this kernel to the given image is called "image filtering". The output obtained after applying the kernel to the image is called the filtered image. Depending on the values in the kernel, it performs different functions like blurring, detecting edges, and so on. The following figure should help you visualize the image filtering operation:

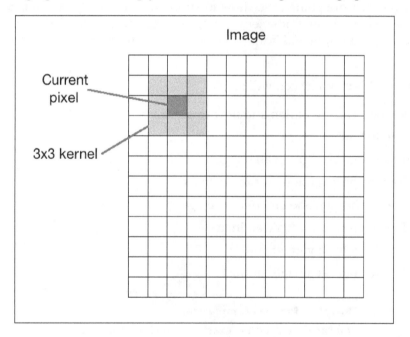

Let's start with the simplest case which is identity kernel. This kernel doesn't really change the input image. If we consider a 3x3 identity kernel, it looks something like the following:

$$I = \begin{bmatrix} 0 & 0 & 0 \\ 0 & 1 & 0 \\ 0 & 0 & 0 \end{bmatrix}$$

# Blurring

Blurring refers to averaging the pixel values within a neighborhood. This is also called a **low pass filter**. A low pass filter is a filter that allows low frequencies and blocks higher frequencies. Now, the next question that comes to our mind is — What does "frequency" mean in an image? Well, in this context, frequency refers to the rate of change of pixel values. So we can say that the sharp edges would be high frequency content because the pixel values change rapidly in that region. Going by that logic, plain areas would be low frequency content. Going by this definition, a low pass filter would try to smoothen the edges.

A simple way to build a low pass filter is by uniformly averaging the values in the neighborhood of a pixel. We can choose the size of the kernel depending on how much we want to smoothen the image, and it will correspondingly have different effects. If you choose a bigger size, then you will be averaging over a larger area. This tends to increase the smoothening effect. Let's see what a 3x3 low pass filter kernel looks like:

$$L = \frac{1}{9} \begin{bmatrix} 1 & 1 & 1 \\ 1 & 1 & 1 \\ 1 & 1 & 1 \end{bmatrix}$$

We are dividing the matrix by 9 because we want the values to sum up to 1. This is called **normalization**, and it's important because we don't want to artificially increase the intensity value at that pixel's location. So you should normalize the kernel before applying it to an image. Normalization is a really important concept, and it is used in a variety of scenarios, so you should read a couple of tutorials online to get a good grasp on it.

Here is the code to apply this low pass filter to an image:

```
import cv2
import numpy as np

img = cv2.imread('input.jpg')
rows, cols = img.shape[:2]

kernel_identity = np.array([[0,0,0], [0,1,0], [0,0,0]])
kernel_3x3 = np.ones((3,3), np.float32) / 9.0
kernel_5x5 = np.ones((5,5), np.float32) / 25.0

cv2.imshow('Original', img)

output = cv2.filter2D(img, -1, kernel_identity)
cv2.imshow('Identity filter', output)

output = cv2.filter2D(img, -1, kernel_3x3)
cv2.imshow('3x3 filter', output)

output = cv2.filter2D(img, -1, kernel_5x5)
cv2.imshow('5x5 filter', output)

cv2.waitKey(0)
```

If you run the preceding code, you will see something like this:

# The size of the kernel versus the blurriness

In the preceding code, we are generating different kernels in the code which are kernel_identity, kernel_3x3, and kernel_5x5. We use the function, filter2D, to apply these kernels to the input image. If you look at the images carefully, you can see that they keep getting blurrier as we increase the kernel size. The reason for this is because when we increase the kernel size, we are averaging over a larger area. This tends to have a larger blurring effect.

An alternative way of doing this would be by using the OpenCV function, blur. If you don't want to generate the kernels yourself, you can just use this function directly. We can call it using the following line of code:

```
output = cv2.blur(img, (3,3))
```

This will apply the 3x3 kernel to the input and give you the output directly.

# Edge detection

The process of edge detection involves detecting sharp edges in the image and producing a binary image as the output. Typically, we draw white lines on a black background to indicate those edges. We can think of edge detection as a high pass filtering operation. A high pass filter allows high frequency content to pass through and blocks the low frequency content. As we discussed earlier, edges are high frequency content. In edge detection, we want to retain these edges and discard everything else. Hence, we should build a kernel that is the equivalent of a high pass filter.

Let's start with a simple edge detection filter known as the Sobel filter. Since edges can occur in both horizontal and vertical directions, the Sobel filter is composed of the following two kernels:

$$S_x = \begin{bmatrix} -1 & 0 & 1 \\ -2 & 0 & 2 \\ -1 & 0 & 1 \end{bmatrix} \qquad S_y = \begin{bmatrix} -1 & -2 & -1 \\ 0 & 0 & 0 \\ 1 & 2 & 1 \end{bmatrix}$$

The kernel on the left detects horizontal edges and the kernel on the right detects vertical edges. OpenCV provides a function to directly apply the Sobel filter to a given image. Here is the code to use Sobel filters to detect edges:

```
import cv2
import numpy as np

img = cv2.imread('input_shapes.png', cv2.IMREAD_GRAYSCALE)
rows, cols = img.shape

sobel_horizontal = cv2.Sobel(img, cv2.CV_64F, 1, 0, ksize=5)
sobel_vertical = cv2.Sobel(img, cv2.CV_64F, 0, 1, ksize=5)

cv2.imshow('Original', img)
cv2.imshow('Sobel horizontal', sobel_horizontal)
cv2.imshow('Sobel vertical', sobel_vertical)

cv2.waitKey(0)
```

The output will look something like the following:

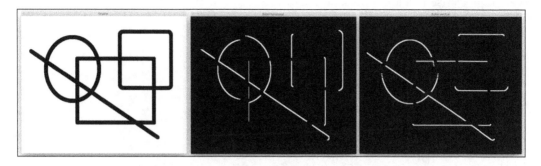

In the preceding figure, the image in the middle is the output of horizontal edge detector, and the image on the right is the vertical edge detector. As we can see here, the Sobel filter detects edges in either a horizontal or vertical direction and it doesn't give us a holistic view of all the edges. To overcome this, we can use the Laplacian filter. The advantage of using this filter is that it uses double derivative in both directions. You can call the function using the following line:

```
laplacian = cv2.Laplacian(img, cv2.CV_64F)
```

The output will look something like the following screenshot:

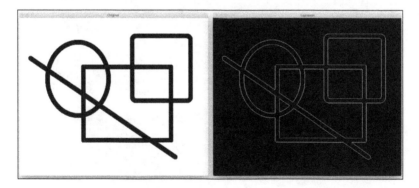

Even though the `Laplacian` kernel worked great in this case, it doesn't always work well. It gives rise to a lot of noise in the output, as shown in the screenshot that follows. This is where the `Canny edge` detector comes in handy:

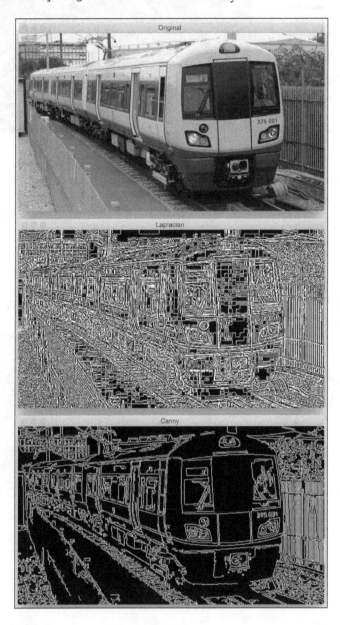

As we can see in the above images, the `Laplacian` kernel gives rise to a noisy output and this is not exactly useful. To overcome this problem, we use the `Canny edge` detector. To use the `Canny edge` detector, we can use the following function:

```
canny = cv2.Canny(img, 50, 240)
```

As we can see, the quality of the Canny edge detector is much better. It takes two numbers as arguments to indicate the thresholds. The second argument is called the low threshold value, and the third argument is called the high threshold value. If the gradient value is above the high threshold value, it is marked as a strong edge. The Canny Edge Detector starts tracking the edge from this point and continues the process until the gradient value falls below the low threshold value. As you increase these thresholds, the weaker edges will be ignored. The output image will be cleaner and sparser. You can play around with the thresholds and see what happens as you increase or decrease their values. The overall formulation is quite deep. You can learn more about it at `http://www.intelligence.tuc.gr/~petrakis/courses/computervision/canny.pdf`

# Motion blur

When we apply the motion blurring effect, it will look like you captured the picture while moving in a particular direction. For example, you can make an image look like it was captured from a moving car.

The input and output images will look like the following ones:

Following is the code to achieve this motion blurring effect:

```
import cv2
import numpy as np

img = cv2.imread('input.jpg')
cv2.imshow('Original', img)

size = 15

# generating the kernel
kernel_motion_blur = np.zeros((size, size))
kernel_motion_blur[int((size-1)/2), :] = np.ones(size)
kernel_motion_blur = kernel_motion_blur / size

# applying the kernel to the input image
output = cv2.filter2D(img, -1, kernel_motion_blur)

cv2.imshow('Motion Blur', output)
cv2.waitKey(0)
```

# Under the hood

We are reading the image as usual. We are then constructing a motion `blur` kernel. A motion blur kernel averages the pixel values in a particular direction. It's like a directional low pass filter. A 3x3 horizontal motion-blurring kernel would look this:

$$M = \begin{bmatrix} 0 & 0 & 0 \\ 1 & 1 & 1 \\ 0 & 0 & 0 \end{bmatrix}$$

This will blur the image in a horizontal direction. You can pick any direction and it will work accordingly. The amount of blurring will depend on the size of the kernel. So, if you want to make the image blurrier, just pick a bigger size for the kernel. To see the full effect, we have taken a 15x15 kernel in the preceding code. We then use `filter2D` to apply this kernel to the input image, to obtain the motion-blurred output.

# Sharpening

Applying the `sharpening` filter will sharpen the edges in the image. This filter is very useful when we want to enhance the edges in an image that's not crisp. Here are some images to give you an idea of what the image `sharpening` process looks like:

As you can see in the preceding figure, the level of sharpening depends on the type of kernel we use. We have a lot of freedom to customize the kernel here, and each kernel will give you a different kind of sharpening. To just sharpen an image, like we are doing in the top right image in the preceding picture, we would use a kernel like this:

$$M = \begin{bmatrix} -1 & -1 & -1 \\ -1 & 9 & -1 \\ -1 & -1 & -1 \end{bmatrix}$$

If we want to do excessive sharpening, like in the bottom left image, we would use the following kernel:

$$M = \begin{bmatrix} 1 & 1 & 1 \\ 1 & -7 & 1 \\ 1 & 1 & 1 \end{bmatrix}$$

But the problem with these two kernels is that the output image looks artificially enhanced. If we want our images to look more natural, we would use an Edge Enhancement filter. The underlying concept remains the same, but we use an approximate Gaussian kernel to build this filter. It will help us smoothen the image when we enhance the edges, thus making the image look more natural.

Here is the code to achieve the effects applied in the preceding screenshot:

```
import cv2
import numpy as np

img = cv2.imread('input.jpg')
cv2.imshow('Original', img)

# generating the kernels
kernel_sharpen_1 = np.array([[-1,-1,-1], [-1,9,-1], [-1,-1,-1]])
kernel_sharpen_2 = np.array([[1,1,1], [1,-7,1], [1,1,1]])
kernel_sharpen_3 = np.array([[-1,-1,-1,-1,-1],
                             [-1,2,2,2,-1],
                             [-1,2,8,2,-1],
                             [-1,2,2,2,-1],
                             [-1,-1,-1,-1,-1]]) / 8.0

# applying different kernels to the input image
output_1 = cv2.filter2D(img, -1, kernel_sharpen_1)
output_2 = cv2.filter2D(img, -1, kernel_sharpen_2)
output_3 = cv2.filter2D(img, -1, kernel_sharpen_3)

cv2.imshow('Sharpening', output_1)
cv2.imshow('Excessive Sharpening', output_2)
cv2.imshow('Edge Enhancement', output_3)
cv2.waitKey(0)
```

If you noticed, in the preceding code, we didn't divide the first two kernels by a normalizing factor. The reason is because the values inside the kernel already sum up to 1, so we are implicitly dividing the matrices by 1.

## Understanding the pattern

You must have noticed a common pattern in image filtering code examples. We build a kernel and then use `filter2D` to get the desired output. That's exactly what's happening in this code example as well! You can play around with the values inside the kernel and see if you can get different visual effects. Make sure that you normalize the kernel before applying it, or else the image will look too bright because you are artificially increasing the pixel values in the image.

# Embossing

An embossing filter will take an image and convert it into an embossed image. We basically take each pixel and replace it with a shadow or a highlight. Let's say we are dealing with a relatively plain region in the image. Here, we need to replace it with plain gray color because there's not much information there. If there is a lot of contrast in a particular region, we will replace it with a white pixel (highlight), or a dark pixel (shadow), depending on the direction in which we are embossing.

This is what it will look like:

Let's take a look at the code and see how to do this:

```
import cv2
import numpy as np

img_emboss_input = cv2.imread('input.jpg')

# generating the kernels
kernel_emboss_1 = np.array([[0,-1,-1],
                            [1,0,-1],
                            [1,1,0]])
kernel_emboss_2 = np.array([[-1,-1,0],
                            [-1,0,1],
                            [0,1,1]])
kernel_emboss_3 = np.array([[1,0,0],
                            [0,0,0],
                            [0,0,-1]])

# converting the image to grayscale
gray_img = cv2.cvtColor(img_emboss_input,cv2.COLOR_BGR2GRAY)

# applying the kernels to the grayscale image and adding the offset
output_1 = cv2.filter2D(gray_img, -1, kernel_emboss_1) + 128
output_2 = cv2.filter2D(gray_img, -1, kernel_emboss_2) + 128
output_3 = cv2.filter2D(gray_img, -1, kernel_emboss_3) + 128

cv2.imshow('Input', img_emboss_input)
cv2.imshow('Embossing - South West', output_1)
cv2.imshow('Embossing - South East', output_2)
cv2.imshow('Embossing - North West', output_3)
cv2.waitKey(0)
```

If you run the preceding code, you will see that the output images are embossed. As we can see from the kernels above, we are just replacing the current pixel value with the difference of the neighboring pixel values in a particular direction. The embossing effect is achieved by offsetting all the pixel values in the image by 128. This operation adds the highlight/shadow effect to the picture.

# Erosion and dilation

**Erosion** and **dilation** are morphological image processing operations. Morphological image processing basically deals with modifying geometric structures in the image. These operations are primarily defined for binary images, but we can also use them on grayscale images. Erosion basically strips out the outermost layer of pixels in a structure, where as dilation adds an extra layer of pixels on a structure.

Let's see what these operations look like:

Following is the code to achieve this:

```
import cv2
import numpy as np

img = cv2.imread('input.png', 0)

kernel = np.ones((5,5), np.uint8)

img_erosion = cv2.erode(img, kernel, iterations=1)
img_dilation = cv2.dilate(img, kernel, iterations=1)

cv2.imshow('Input', img)
cv2.imshow('Erosion', img_erosion)
cv2.imshow('Dilation', img_dilation)

cv2.waitKey(0)
```

# Afterthought

OpenCV provides functions to directly erode and dilate an image. They are called erode and dilate, respectively. The interesting thing to note is the third argument in these two functions. The number of iterations will determine how much you want to erode/dilate a given image. It basically applies the operation successively to the resultant image. You can take a sample image and play around with this parameter to see what the results look like.

# Creating a vignette filter

Using all the information we have, let's see if we can create a nice vignette filter. The output will look something like the following:

Here is the code to achieve this effect:

```
import cv2
import numpy as np

img = cv2.imread('input.jpg')
rows, cols = img.shape[:2]

# generating vignette mask using Gaussian kernels
kernel_x = cv2.getGaussianKernel(cols,200)
kernel_y = cv2.getGaussianKernel(rows,200)
kernel = kernel_y * kernel_x.T
```

```
mask = 255 * kernel / np.linalg.norm(kernel)
output = np.copy(img)

# applying the mask to each channel in the input image
for i in range(3):
    output[:,:,i] = output[:,:,i] * mask

cv2.imshow('Original', img)
cv2.imshow('Vignette', output)
cv2.waitKey(0)
```

# What's happening underneath?

The `Vignette` filter basically focuses the brightness on a particular part of the image and the other parts look faded. In order to achieve this, we need to filter out each channel in the image using a Gaussian kernel. OpenCV provides a function to do this, which is called `getGaussianKernel`. We need to build a 2D kernel whose size matches the size of the image. The second parameter of the function, `getGaussianKernel`, is interesting. It is the standard deviation of the Gaussian and it controls the radius of the bright central region. You can play around with this parameter and see how it affects the output.

Once we build the 2D kernel, we need to build a mask by normalizing this kernel and scaling it up, as shown in the following line:

```
mask = 255 * kernel / np.linalg.norm(kernel)
```

This is an important step because if you don't scale it up, the image will look black. This happens because all the pixel values will be close to 0 after you superimpose the mask on the input image. After this, we iterate through all the color channels and apply the mask to each channel.

# How do we move the focus around?

We now know how to create a `vignette` filter that focuses on the center of the image. Let's say we want to achieve the same `vignette` effect, but we want to focus on a different region in the image, as shown in the following figure:

All we need to do is build a bigger Gaussian kernel and make sure that the peak coincides with the region of interest. Following is the code to achieve this:

```
import cv2
import numpy as np

img = cv2.imread('input.jpg')
rows, cols = img.shape[:2]

# generating vignette mask using Gaussian kernels
kernel_x = cv2.getGaussianKernel(int(1.5*cols),200)
kernel_y = cv2.getGaussianKernel(int(1.5*rows),200)
kernel = kernel_y * kernel_x.T
mask = 255 * kernel / np.linalg.norm(kernel)
mask = mask[int(0.5*rows):, int(0.5*cols):]
output = np.copy(img)
```

```
# applying the mask to each channel in the input image
for i in range(3):
    output[:,:,i] = output[:,:,i] * mask

cv2.imshow('Input', img)
cv2.imshow('Vignette with shifted focus', output)

cv2.waitKey(0)
```

# Enhancing the contrast in an image

Whenever we capture images in low-light conditions, the images turn out to be dark. This typically happens when you capture images in the evening or in a dimly lit room. You must have seen this happen many times! The reason this happens is because the pixel values tend to concentrate near 0 when we capture the images under such conditions. When this happens, a lot of details in the image are not clearly visible to the human eye. The human eye likes contrast, and so we need to adjust the contrast to make the image look nice and pleasant. A lot of cameras and photo applications implicitly do this already. We use a process called **Histogram Equalization** to achieve this.

To give an example, this is what it looks like before and after contrast enhancement:

As we can see here, the input image on the left is really dark. To rectify this, we need to adjust the pixel values so that they are spread across the entire spectrum of values, that is, between 0 and 255.

Following is the code for adjusting the pixel values:

```
import cv2
import numpy as np

img = cv2.imread('input.jpg', 0)

# equalize the histogram of the input image
histeq = cv2.equalizeHist(img)

cv2.imshow('Input', img)
cv2.imshow('Histogram equalized', histeq)
cv2.waitKey(0)
```

Histogram equalization is applicable to grayscale images. OpenCV provides a function, equalizeHist, to achieve this effect. As we can see here, the code is pretty straightforward, where we read the image and equalize its histogram to adjust the contrast of the image.

# How do we handle color images?

Now that we know how to equalize the histogram of a grayscale image, you might be wondering how to handle color images. The thing about histogram equalization is that it's a nonlinear process. So, we cannot just separate out the three channels in an RGB image, equalize the histogram separately, and combine them later to form the output image. The concept of histogram equalization is only applicable to the intensity values in the image. So, we have to make sure not to modify the color information when we do this.

In order to handle the histogram equalization of color images, we need to convert it to a color space where intensity is separated from the color information. YUV is a good example of such a color space. Once we convert it to YUV, we just need to equalize the Y-channel and combine it with the other two channels to get the output image.

Following is an example of what it looks like:

Here is the code to achieve histogram equalization for color images:

```
import cv2
import numpy as np

img = cv2.imread('input.jpg')

img_yuv = cv2.cvtColor(img, cv2.COLOR_BGR2YUV)

# equalize the histogram of the Y channel
img_yuv[:,:,0] = cv2.equalizeHist(img_yuv[:,:,0])

# convert the YUV image back to RGB format
img_output = cv2.cvtColor(img_yuv, cv2.COLOR_YUV2BGR)

cv2.imshow('Color input image', img)
cv2.imshow('Histogram equalized', img_output)

cv2.waitKey(0)
```

# Summary

In this chapter, we learned how to use image filters to apply cool visual effects to images. We discussed the fundamental image processing operators and how we can use them to build various things. We learnt how to detect edges using various methods. We understood the importance of 2D convolution and how we can use it in different scenarios. We discussed how to smoothen, motion-blur, sharpen, emboss, erode, and dilate an image. We learned how to create a vignette filter, and how we can change the region of focus as well. We discussed contrast enhancement and how we can use histogram equalization to achieve it. In the next chapter, we will discuss how to cartoonize a given image.

# 3
# Cartoonizing an Image

In this chapter, we are going to learn how to convert an image into a cartoon-like image. We will learn how to access the webcam and take keyboard/mouse inputs during a live video stream. We will also learn about some advanced image filters and see how we can use them to cartoonize an image.

By the end of this chapter, you will know:

- How to access the webcam
- How to take keyboard and mouse inputs during a live video stream
- How to create an interactive application
- How to use advanced image filters
- How to cartoonize an image

## Accessing the webcam

We can build very interesting applications using the live video stream from the webcam. OpenCV provides a video capture object which handles everything related to opening and closing of the webcam. All we need to do is create that object and keep reading frames from it.

The following code will open the webcam, capture the frames, scale them down by a factor of 2, and then display them in a window. You can press the *Esc* key to exit.

```
import cv2

cap = cv2.VideoCapture(0)

# Check if the webcam is opened correctly
if not cap.isOpened():
```

```
        raise IOError("Cannot open webcam")

    while True:
        ret, frame = cap.read()
        frame = cv2.resize(frame, None, fx=0.5, fy=0.5, interpolation=cv2.
    INTER_AREA)
        cv2.imshow('Input', frame)

        c = cv2.waitKey(1)
        if c == 27:
            break

    cap.release()
    cv2.destroyAllWindows()
```

# Under the hood

As we can see in the preceding code, we use OpenCV's `VideoCapture` function to create the video capture object cap. Once it's created, we start an infinite loop and keep reading frames from the webcam until we encounter a keyboard interrupt. In the first line within the while loop, we have the following line:

```
    ret, frame = cap.read()
```

Here, `ret` is a Boolean value returned by the `read` function, and it indicates whether or not the frame was captured successfully. If the frame is captured correctly, it's stored in the variable `frame`. This loop will keep running until we press the *Esc* key. So we keep checking for a keyboard interrupt in the following line:

```
    if c == 27:
```

As we know, the ASCII value of *Esc* is 27. Once we encounter it, we break the loop and release the video capture object. The line `cap.release()` is important because it gracefully closes the webcam.

# Keyboard inputs

Now that we know how to capture a live video stream from the webcam, let's see how to use the keyboard to interact with the window displaying the video stream.

```
    import argparse

    import cv2

    def argument_parser():
```

```
    parser = argparse.ArgumentParser(description="Change color space
of the \
            input video stream using keyboard controls. The control
keys are: \
            Grayscale - 'g', YUV - 'y', HSV - 'h'")
    return parser

if __name__=='__main__':
    args = argument_parser().parse_args()

    cap = cv2.VideoCapture(0)

    # Check if the webcam is opened correctly
    if not cap.isOpened():
        raise IOError("Cannot open webcam")

    cur_char = -1
    prev_char = -1

    while True:
        # Read the current frame from webcam
        ret, frame = cap.read()

        # Resize the captured image
        frame = cv2.resize(frame, None, fx=0.5, fy=0.5,
interpolation=cv2.INTER_AREA)

        c = cv2.waitKey(1)

        if c == 27:
            break

        if c > -1 and c != prev_char:
            cur_char = c
        prev_char = c

        if cur_char == ord('g'):
            output = cv2.cvtColor(frame, cv2.COLOR_BGR2GRAY)
        elif cur_char == ord('y'):
            output = cv2.cvtColor(frame, cv2.COLOR_BGR2YUV)

        elif cur_char == ord('h'):
            output = cv2.cvtColor(frame, cv2.COLOR_BGR2HSV)
```

```
    else:
        output = frame

    cv2.imshow('Webcam', output)

cap.release()
cv2.destroyAllWindows()
```

# Interacting with the application

This program will display the input video stream and wait for the keyboard input to change the color space. If you run the previous program, you will see the window displaying the input video stream from the webcam. If you press *G*, you will see that the color space of the input stream gets converted to grayscale. If you press *Y*, the input stream will be converted to YUV color space. Similarly, if you press *H*, you will see the image being converted to HSV color space.

As we know, we use the function waitKey() to listen to the keyboard events. As and when we encounter different keystrokes, we take appropriate actions. The reason we are using the function ord() is because waitKey() returns the ASCII value of the keyboard input; thus, we need to convert the characters into their ASCII form before checking their values.

# Mouse inputs

In this section, we will see how to use the mouse to interact with the display window. Let's start with something simple. We will write a program that will detect the quadrant in which the mouse click was detected. Once we detect it, we will highlight that quadrant.

```
import cv2
import numpy as np

def detect_quadrant(event, x, y, flags, param):
    if event == cv2.EVENT_LBUTTONDOWN:
        if x > width/2:
            if y > height/2:
                point_top_left = (int(width/2), int(height/2))
                point_bottom_right = (width-1, height-1)
            else:
                point_top_left = (int(width/2), 0)
                point_bottom_right = (width-1, int(height/2))
```

```
        else:
            if y > height/2:
                point_top_left = (0, int(height/2))
                point_bottom_right = (int(width/2), height-1)
            else:
                point_top_left = (0, 0)
                point_bottom_right = (int(width/2), int(height/2))

        cv2.rectangle(img, (0,0), (width-1,height-1), (255,255,255),
-1)
        cv2.rectangle(img, point_top_left, point_bottom_right,
(0,100,0), -1)

if __name__=='__main__':
    width, height = 640, 480
    img = 255 * np.ones((height, width, 3), dtype=np.uint8)
    cv2.namedWindow('Input window')
    cv2.setMouseCallback('Input window', detect_quadrant)

    while True:
        cv2.imshow('Input window', img)
        c = cv2.waitKey(10)
        if c == 27:
            break

    cv2.destroyAllWindows()
```

The output will look something like the following image:

# What's happening underneath?

Let's start with the main function in this program. We create a white image on which we are going to click using the mouse. We then create a named window and bind the mouse callback function to this window. Mouse callback function is basically the function that will be called when a mouse event is detected. There are many kinds of mouse events such as clicking, double-clicking, dragging, and so on. In our case, we just want to detect a mouse click. In the function detect_quadrant, we check the first input argument event to see what action was performed. OpenCV provides a set of predefined events, and we can call them using specific keywords. If you want to see a list of all the mouse events, you can go to the Python shell and type the following:

```
>>> import cv2
>>> print [x for x in dir(cv2) if x.startswith('EVENT')]
```

The second and third arguments in the function detect_quadrant provide the X and Y coordinates of the mouse click event. Once we know these coordinates, it's pretty straightforward to determine what quadrant it's in. With this information, we just go ahead and draw a rectangle with the specified color, using cv2.rectangle(). This is a very handy function that takes the top left point and the bottom right point to draw a rectangle on an image with the specified color.

# Interacting with a live video stream

Let's see how we can use the mouse to interact with live video stream from the webcam. We can use the mouse to select a region and then apply the "negative film" effect on that region, as shown next:

In the following program, we will capture the video stream from the webcam, select a region of interest with the mouse, and then apply the effect:

```python
import cv2
import numpy as np

def draw_rectangle(event, x, y, flags, params):
    global x_init, y_init, drawing, top_left_pt, bottom_right_pt

    if event == cv2.EVENT_LBUTTONDOWN:
        drawing = True
        x_init, y_init = x, y

    elif event == cv2.EVENT_MOUSEMOVE:
        if drawing:
            top_left_pt = (min(x_init, x), min(y_init, y))
            bottom_right_pt = (max(x_init, x), max(y_init, y))
            img[y_init:y, x_init:x] = 255 - img[y_init:y, x_init:x]

    elif event == cv2.EVENT_LBUTTONUP:
        drawing = False
        top_left_pt = (min(x_init, x), min(y_init, y))
        bottom_right_pt = (max(x_init, x), max(y_init, y))
        img[y_init:y, x_init:x] = 255 - img[y_init:y, x_init:x]

if __name__=='__main__':
    drawing = False
    top_left_pt, bottom_right_pt = (-1,-1), (-1,-1)

    cap = cv2.VideoCapture(0)

    # Check if the webcam is opened correctly
    if not cap.isOpened():
        raise IOError("Cannot open webcam")

    cv2.namedWindow('Webcam')
    cv2.setMouseCallback('Webcam', draw_rectangle)

    while True:
        ret, frame = cap.read()
        img = cv2.resize(frame, None, fx=0.5, fy=0.5,
interpolation=cv2.INTER_AREA)
        (x0,y0), (x1,y1) = top_left_pt, bottom_right_pt
        img[y0:y1, x0:x1] = 255 - img[y0:y1, x0:x1]
```

```
            cv2.imshow('Webcam', img)

            c = cv2.waitKey(1)
            if c == 27:
                break

        cap.release()
        cv2.destroyAllWindows()
```

If you run the preceding program, you will see a window displaying the video stream. You can just draw a rectangle on the window using your mouse and you will see that region being converted to its "negative".

## How did we do it?

As we can see in the main function of the program, we initialize a video capture object. We then bind the function `draw_rectangle` with the mouse callback in the following line:

```
    cv2.setMouseCallback('Webcam', draw_rectangle)
```

We then start an infinite loop and start capturing the video stream. Let's see what is happening in the function `draw_rectangle`. Whenever we draw a rectangle using the mouse, we basically have to detect three types of mouse events: mouse click, mouse movement, and mouse button release. This is exactly what we do in this function. Whenever we detect a mouse click event, we initialize the top left point of the rectangle. As we move the mouse, we select the region of interest by keeping the current position as the bottom right point of the rectangle.

Once we have the region of interest, we just invert the pixels to apply the "negative film" effect. We subtract the current pixel value from 255 and this gives us the desired effect. When the mouse movement stops and button-up event is detected, we stop updating the bottom right position of the rectangle. We just keep displaying this image until another mouse click event is detected.

## Cartoonizing an image

Now that we know how to handle the webcam and keyboard/mouse inputs, let's go ahead and see how to convert a picture into a cartoon-like image. We can either convert an image into a sketch or a colored cartoon image.

Following is an example of what a sketch will look like:

If you apply the cartoonizing effect to the color image, it will look something like this next image:

Let's see how to achieve this:

```python
import cv2
import numpy as np

def cartoonize_image(img, ds_factor=4, sketch_mode=False):
    # Convert image to grayscale
    img_gray = cv2.cvtColor(img, cv2.COLOR_BGR2GRAY)

    # Apply median filter to the grayscale image
    img_gray = cv2.medianBlur(img_gray, 7)

    # Detect edges in the image and threshold it
    edges = cv2.Laplacian(img_gray, cv2.CV_8U, ksize=5)
    ret, mask = cv2.threshold(edges, 100, 255, cv2.THRESH_BINARY_INV)

    # 'mask' is the sketch of the image
    if sketch_mode:
        return cv2.cvtColor(mask, cv2.COLOR_GRAY2BGR)

    # Resize the image to a smaller size for faster computation
    img_small = cv2.resize(img, None, fx=1.0/ds_factor, fy=1.0/ds_factor, interpolation=cv2.INTER_AREA)
    num_repetitions = 10
    sigma_color = 5
    sigma_space = 7
    size = 5

    # Apply bilateral filter the image multiple times
    for i in range(num_repetitions):
        img_small = cv2.bilateralFilter(img_small, size, sigma_color, sigma_space)

    img_output = cv2.resize(img_small, None, fx=ds_factor, fy=ds_factor, interpolation=cv2.INTER_LINEAR)

    dst = np.zeros(img_gray.shape)

    # Add the thick boundary lines to the image using 'AND' operator
    dst = cv2.bitwise_and(img_output, img_output, mask=mask)
    return dst
```

```python
if __name__=='__main__':
    cap = cv2.VideoCapture(0)

    cur_char = -1
    prev_char = -1

    while True:
        ret, frame = cap.read()
        frame = cv2.resize(frame, None, fx=0.5, fy=0.5,
interpolation=cv2.INTER_AREA)

        c = cv2.waitKey(1)
        if c == 27:
            break

        if c > -1 and c != prev_char:
            cur_char = c
        prev_char = c

        if cur_char == ord('s'):
            cv2.imshow('Cartoonize', cartoonize_image(frame, sketch_
mode=True))
        elif cur_char == ord('c'):
            cv2.imshow('Cartoonize', cartoonize_image(frame, sketch_
mode=False))
        else:
            cv2.imshow('Cartoonize', frame)

    cap.release()
    cv2.destroyAllWindows()
```

# Deconstructing the code

When you run the preceding program, you will see a window with a video stream from the webcam. If you press *S*, the video stream will change to sketch mode and you will see its pencil-like outline. If you press *C*, you will see the color-cartoonized version of the input stream. If you press any other key, it will return to the normal mode.

Let's look at the function `cartoonize_image` and see how we did it. We first convert the image to a grayscale image and run it through a median filter. Median filters are very good at removing salt and pepper noise. This is the kind of noise where you see isolated black or white pixels in the image. It is common in webcams and mobile cameras, so we need to filter it out before we proceed further. To give an example, look at the following images:

As we see in the input image, there are a lot of isolated green pixels. They are lowering the quality of the image and we need to get rid of them. This is where the median filter comes in handy. We just look at the NxN neighborhood around each pixel and pick the median value of those numbers. Since the isolated pixels in this case have high values, taking the median value will get rid of these values and also smoothen the image. As you can see in the output image, the median filter got rid of all those isolated pixels and the image looks clean. Following is the code to do it:

```
import cv2
import numpy as np

img = cv2.imread('input.png')
output = cv2.medianBlur(img, 7)
cv2.imshow('Input', img)
cv2.imshow('Median filter', output)
cv2.waitKey()
```

The code is pretty straightforward. We just use the function `medianBlur` to apply the median filter to the input image. The second argument in this function specifies the size of the kernel we are using. The size of the kernel is related to the neighborhood size that we need to consider. You can play around with this parameter and see how it affects the output.

Coming back to `cartoonize_image`, we proceed to detect the edges on the grayscale image. We need to know where the edges are so that we can create the pencil-line effect. Once we detect the edges, we threshold them so that things become black and white, both literally and metaphorically!

In the next step, we check if the sketch mode is enabled. If it is, then we just convert it into a color image and return it. What if we want the lines to be thicker? Let's say we want to see something like the following image:

As you can see, the lines are thicker than before. To achieve this, replace the `if` code block with the following piece of code:

```
if sketch_mode:
    img_sketch = cv2.cvtColor(mask, cv2.COLOR_GRAY2BGR)
    kernel = np.ones((3,3), np.uint8)
    img_eroded = cv2.erode(img_sketch, kernel, iterations=1)
    return cv2.medianBlur(img_eroded, 5)
```

We are using the erode function with a 3x3 kernel here. The reason we have this in place is because it gives us a chance to play with the thickness of the line drawing. Now you might ask that if we want to increase the thickness of something, shouldn't we be using dilation? Well, the reasoning is right, but there is a small twist here. Note that the foreground is black and the background is white. Erosion and dilation treat white pixels as foreground and black pixels as background. So if we want to increase the thickness of the black foreground, we need to use erosion. After we apply erosion, we just use the median filter to clear out the noise and get the final output.

In the next step, we use bilateral filtering to smoothen the image. Bilateral filtering is an interesting concept and its performance is much better than a Gaussian filter. The good thing about bilateral filtering is that it preserves the edges, whereas the Gaussian filter smoothens everything out equally. To compare and contrast, let's look at the following input image:

Let's apply the Gaussian filter to the previous image:

Now, let's apply the bilateral filter to the input image:

As you can see, the quality is better if we use the bilateral filter. The image looks smooth and the edges look nice and sharp! The code to achieve this is given next:

```
import cv2
import numpy as np

img = cv2.imread('input.jpg')
```

```
img_gaussian = cv2.GaussianBlur(img, (13,13), 0)
img_bilateral = cv2.bilateralFilter(img, 13, 70, 50)

cv2.imshow('Input', img)
cv2.imshow('Gaussian filter', img_gaussian)
cv2.imshow('Bilateral filter', img_bilateral)
cv2.waitKey()
```

If you closely observe the two outputs, you can see that the edges in the Gaussian filtered image look blurred. Usually, we just want to smoothen the rough areas in the image and keep the edges intact. This is where the bilateral filter comes in handy. The Gaussian filter just looks at the immediate neighborhood and averages the pixel values using a Gaussian kernel. The bilateral filter takes this concept to the next level by averaging only those pixels that are similar to each other in intensity. It also takes a color neighborhood metric to see if it can replace the current pixel that is similar in intensity as well. If you look the function call:

```
img_small = cv2.bilateralFilter(img_small, size, sigma_color,
sigma_space)
```

The last two arguments here specify the color and space neighborhood. This is the reason the edges look crisp in the output of the bilateral filter. We run this filter multiple times on the image to smoothen it out, to make it look like a cartoon. We then superimpose the pencil-like mask on top of this color image to create a cartoon-like effect.

# Summary

In this chapter, we learnt how to access the webcam. We discussed how to take the keyboard and mouse inputs during live video stream. We used this knowledge to create an interactive application. We discussed the median and bilateral filters, and talked about the advantages of the bilateral filter over the Gaussian filter. We used all these principles to convert the input image into a sketch-like image, and then cartoonized it.

In the next chapter, we will learn how to detect different body parts in static images as well as in live videos.

# 4
# Detecting and Tracking Different Body Parts

In this chapter, we are going to learn how to detect and track different body parts in a live video stream. We will start by discussing the face detection pipeline and how it's built from the ground up. We will learn how to use this framework to detect and track other body parts, such as eyes, ears, mouth, and nose.

By the end of this chapter, you will know:

- How to use Haar cascades
- What are integral images
- What is adaptive boosting
- How to detect and track faces in a live video stream
- How to detect and track eyes in a live video stream
- How to automatically overlay sunglasses on top of a person's face
- How to detect ears, nose, and mouth
- How to detect pupils using shape analysis

## Using Haar cascades to detect things

When we say Haar cascades, we are actually talking about cascade classifiers based on Haar features. To understand what this means, we need to take a step back and understand why we need this in the first place. Back in 2001, Paul Viola and Michael Jones came up with a very effective object detection method in their seminal paper. It has become one of the major landmarks in the field of machine learning.

In their paper, they have described a machine learning technique where a boosted cascade of simple classifiers is used to get an overall classifier that performs really well. This way, we can circumvent the process of building a single complex classifier that performs with high accuracy. The reason this is so amazing is because building a robust single-step classifier is a computationally intensive process. Besides, we need a lot of training data to build such a classifier. The model ends up becoming complex and the performance might not be up to the mark.

Let's say we want to detect an object like, say, a pineapple. To solve this, we need to build a machine learning system that will learn what a pineapple looks like. It should be able to tell us if an unknown image contains a pineapple or not. To achieve something like this, we need to train our system. In the realm of machine learning, we have a lot of methods available to train a system. It's a lot like training a dog, except that it won't fetch the ball for you! To train our system, we take a lot of pineapple and non-pineapple images, and then feed them into the system. Here, pineapple images are called positive images and the non-pineapple images are called negative images.

As far as the training is concerned, there are a lot of routes available. But all the traditional techniques are computationally intensive and result in complex models. We cannot use these models to build a real time system. Hence, we need to keep the classifier simple. But if we keep the classifier simple, it will not be accurate. The trade off between speed and accuracy is common in machine learning. We overcome this problem by building a set of simple classifiers and then cascading them together to form a unified classifier that's robust. To make sure that the overall classifier works well, we need to get creative in the cascading step. This is one of the main reasons why the **Viola-Jones** method is so effective.

Coming to the topic of face detection, let's see how to train a system to detect faces. If we want to build a machine learning system, we first need to extract features from all the images. In our case, the machine learning algorithms will use these features to learn what a face looks like. We use Haar features to build our feature vectors. Haar features are simple summations and differences of patches across the image. We do this at multiple image sizes to make sure our system is scale invariant.

 If you are curious, you can learn more about the formulation at http://www.cs.ubc.ca/~lowe/425/slides/13-ViolaJones.pdf

Once we extract these features, we pass it through a cascade of classifiers. We just check all the different rectangular sub-regions and keep discarding the ones that don't have faces in them. This way, we arrive at the final answer quickly to see if a given rectangle contains a face or not.

# What are integral images?

If we want to compute Haar features, we will have to compute the summations of many different rectangular regions within the image. If we want to effectively build the feature set, we need to compute these summations at multiple scales. This is a very expensive process! If we want to build a real time system, we cannot spend so many cycles in computing these sums. So we use something called integral images.

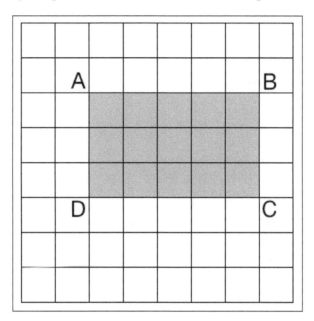

To compute the sum of any rectangle in the image, we don't need to go through all the elements in that rectangular area. Let's say AP indicates the sum of all the elements in the rectangle formed by the top left point and the point P in the image as the two diagonally opposite corners. So now, if we want to compute the area of the rectangle ABCD, we can use the following formula:

*Area of the rectangle ABCD = AC – (AB + AD - AA)*

Why do we care about this particular formula? As we discussed earlier, extracting Haar features includes computing the areas of a large number of rectangles in the image at multiple scales. A lot of those computations are repetitive and the overall process is very slow. In fact, it is so slow that we cannot afford to run anything in real time. That's the reason we use this formulation! The good thing about this approach is that we don't have to recalculate anything. All the values for the areas on the right hand side of this equation are already available. So we just use them to compute the area of any given rectangle and extract the features.

# Detecting and tracking faces

OpenCV provides a nice face detection framework. We just need to load the cascade file and use it to detect the faces in an image. Let's see how to do it:

```python
import cv2
import numpy as np

face_cascade =
cv2.CascadeClassifier('./cascade_files/haarcascade_frontalface_alt.
xml')

cap = cv2.VideoCapture(0)
scaling_factor = 0.5

while True:
    ret, frame = cap.read()
    frame = cv2.resize(frame, None, fx=scaling_factor,
fy=scaling_factor, interpolation=cv2.INTER_AREA)
    gray = cv2.cvtColor(frame, cv2.COLOR_BGR2GRAY)

    face_rects = face_cascade.detectMultiScale(gray, 1.3, 5)
    for (x,y,w,h) in face_rects:
        cv2.rectangle(frame, (x,y), (x+w,y+h), (0,255,0), 3)

    cv2.imshow('Face Detector', frame)

    c = cv2.waitKey(1)
    if c == 27:
        break

cap.release()
cv2.destroyAllWindows()
```

If you run the above code, it will look something like the following image:

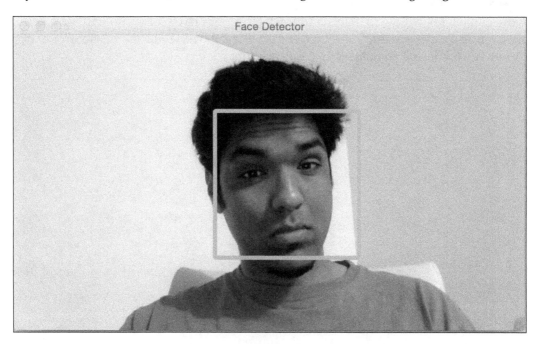

# Understanding it better

We need a classifier model that can be used to detect the faces in an image. OpenCV provides an xml file that can be used for this purpose. We use the function CascadeClassifier to load the xml file. Once we start capturing the input frames from the webcam, we convert it to grayscale and use the function detectMultiScale to get the bounding boxes for all the faces in the current image. The second argument in this function specifies the jump in the scaling factor. As in, if we don't find an image in the current scale, the next size to check will be, in our case, 1.3 times bigger than the current size. The last parameter is a threshold that specifies the number of adjacent rectangles needed to keep the current rectangle. It can be used to increase the robustness of the face detector.

# Fun with faces

Now that we know how to detect and track faces, let's have some fun with it. When we capture a video stream from the webcam, we can overlay funny masks on top of our faces. It will look something like this next image:

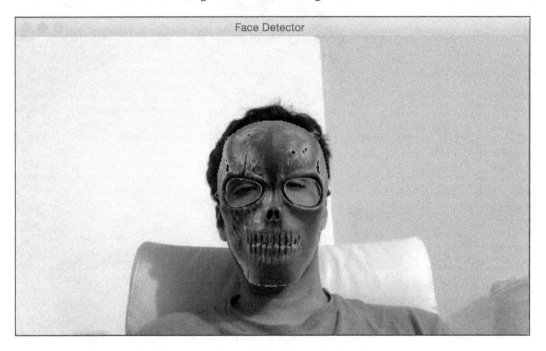

If you are a fan of Hannibal, you can try this next one:

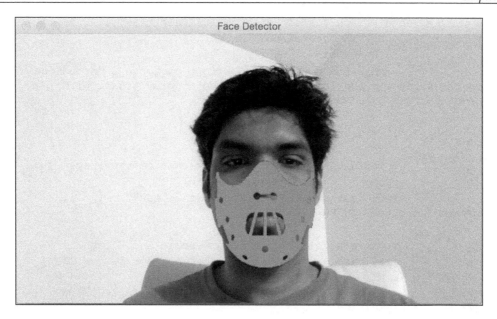

Let's look at the code to see how to overlay the skull mask on top of the face in the input video stream:

```python
import cv2
import numpy as np

face_cascade =
cv2.CascadeClassifier('./cascade_files/haarcascade_frontalface_alt.
xml')

face_mask = cv2.imread('mask_hannibal.png')
h_mask, w_mask = face_mask.shape[:2]

if face_cascade.empty():
    raise IOError('Unable to load the face cascade classifier
xml file')

cap = cv2.VideoCapture(0)
scaling_factor = 0.5

while True:
    ret, frame = cap.read()
    frame = cv2.resize(frame, None, fx=scaling_factor,
fy=scaling_factor, interpolation=cv2.INTER_AREA)
    gray = cv2.cvtColor(frame, cv2.COLOR_BGR2GRAY)
```

```
    face_rects = face_cascade.detectMultiScale(gray, 1.3, 5)
    for (x,y,w,h) in face_rects:
        if h > 0 and w > 0:
            # Adjust the height and weight parameters depending
on the sizes and the locations. You need to play around with
these to make sure you get it right.
            h, w = int(1.4*h), int(1.0*w)
            y -= 0.1*h

            # Extract the region of interest from the image
            frame_roi = frame[y:y+h, x:x+w]
            face_mask_small = cv2.resize(face_mask, (w, h),
interpolation=cv2.INTER_AREA)

            # Convert color image to grayscale and threshold it
            gray_mask = cv2.cvtColor(face_mask_small, cv2.COLOR_
BGR2GRAY)
            ret, mask = cv2.threshold(gray_mask, 180, 255,
cv2.THRESH_BINARY_INV)

            # Create an inverse mask
            mask_inv = cv2.bitwise_not(mask)

            # Use the mask to extract the face mask region of
interest
            masked_face = cv2.bitwise_and(face_mask_small, face_mask_
small, mask=mask)

            # Use the inverse mask to get the remaining part of
the image
            masked_frame = cv2.bitwise_and(frame_roi,
frame_roi, mask=mask_inv)

            # add the two images to get the final output
            frame[y:y+h, x:x+w] = cv2.add(masked_face,
masked_frame)

    cv2.imshow('Face Detector', frame)

    c = cv2.waitKey(1)
    if c == 27:
        break

cap.release()
cv2.destroyAllWindows()
```

# Under the hood

Just like before, we first load the face cascade classifier xml file. The face detection steps work as usual. We start the infinite loop and keep detecting the face in every frame. Once we know where the face is, we need to modify the coordinates a bit to make sure the mask fits properly. This manipulation process is subjective and depends on the mask in question. Different masks require different levels of adjustments to make it look more natural. We extract the region-of-interest from the input frame in the following line:

```
frame_roi = frame[y:y+h, x:x+w]
```

Now that we have the required region-of-interest, we need to overlay the mask on top of this. So we resize the input mask to make sure it fits in this region-of-interest. The input mask has a white background. So if we just overlay this on top of the region-of-interest, it will look unnatural because of the white background. We need to overlay only the skull-mask pixels and the remaining area should be transparent.

So in the next step, we create a mask by thresholding the skull image. Since the background is white, we threshold the image so that any pixel with an intensity value greater than 180 becomes 0, and everything else becomes 255. As far as the frame region-of-interest is concerned, we need to black out everything in this mask region. We can do that by simply using the inverse of the mask we just created. Once we have the masked versions of the skull image and the input region-of-interest, we just add them up to get the final image.

# Detecting eyes

Now that we understand how to detect faces, we can generalize the concept to detect other body parts too. It's important to understand that Viola-Jones framework can be applied to any object. The accuracy and robustness will depend on the uniqueness of the object. For example, a human face has very unique characteristics, so it's easy to train our system to be robust. On the other hand, an object like towel is too generic, and there are no distinguishing characteristics as such; so it's more difficult to build a robust towel detector.

Let's see how to build an eye detector:

```
import cv2
import numpy as np

face_cascade = cv2.CascadeClassifier('./cascade_files/haarcascade_
frontalface_alt.xml')
eye_cascade = cv2.CascadeClassifier('./cascade_files/haarcascade_eye.
xml')
```

```
if face_cascade.empty():
  raise IOError('Unable to load the face cascade classifier xml file')

if eye_cascade.empty():
  raise IOError('Unable to load the eye cascade classifier xml file')

cap = cv2.VideoCapture(0)
ds_factor = 0.5

while True:
    ret, frame = cap.read()
    frame = cv2.resize(frame, None, fx=ds_factor, fy=ds_factor,
interpolation=cv2.INTER_AREA)
    gray = cv2.cvtColor(frame, cv2.COLOR_BGR2GRAY)

    faces = face_cascade.detectMultiScale(gray, 1.3, 5)
    for (x,y,w,h) in faces:
        roi_gray = gray[y:y+h, x:x+w]
        roi_color = frame[y:y+h, x:x+w]
        eyes = eye_cascade.detectMultiScale(roi_gray)
        for (x_eye,y_eye,w_eye,h_eye) in eyes:
            center = (int(x_eye + 0.5*w_eye), int(y_eye + 0.5*h_eye))
            radius = int(0.3 * (w_eye + h_eye))
            color = (0, 255, 0)
            thickness = 3
            cv2.circle(roi_color, center, radius, color, thickness)

    cv2.imshow('Eye Detector', frame)

    c = cv2.waitKey(1)
    if c == 27:
        break

cap.release()
cv2.destroyAllWindows()
```

If you run this program, the output will look something like the following image:

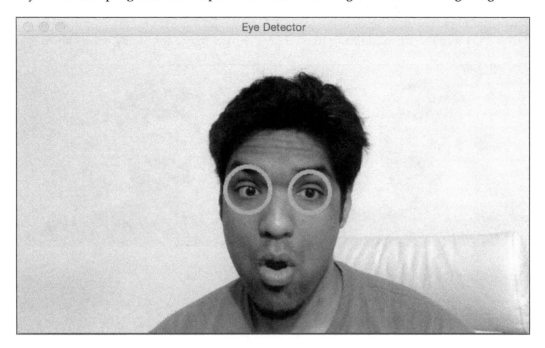

# Afterthought

If you notice, the program looks very similar to the face detection program. Along with loading the face detection cascade classifier, we load the eye detection cascade classifier as well. Technically, we don't need to use the face detector. But we know that eyes are always on somebody's face. We use this information and search for eyes only in the relevant region of interest, that is the face. We first detect the face, and then run the eye detector on this sub-image. This way, it's faster and more efficient.

# Fun with eyes

Now that we know how to detect eyes in an image, let's see if we can do something fun with it. We can do something like what is shown in the following screenshot:

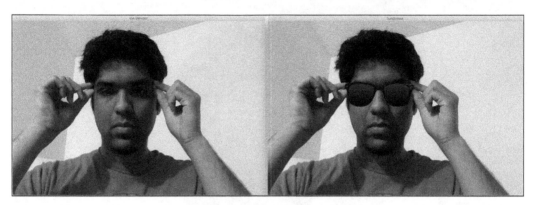

Let's look at the code to see how to do something like this:

```
import cv2
import numpy as np

face_cascade =
cv2.CascadeClassifier('./cascade_files/haarcascade_frontalface_alt.
xml')
eye_cascade = cv2.CascadeClassifier('./cascade_files/haarcascade_eye.
xml')

if face_cascade.empty():
  raise IOError('Unable to load the face cascade classifier
xml file')

if eye_cascade.empty():
  raise IOError('Unable to load the eye cascade classifier xml
file')

img = cv2.imread('input.jpg')
sunglasses_img = cv2.imread('sunglasses.jpg')

gray = cv2.cvtColor(img, cv2.COLOR_BGR2GRAY)

centers = []
faces = face_cascade.detectMultiScale(gray, 1.3, 5)

for (x,y,w,h) in faces:
```

```
    roi_gray = gray[y:y+h, x:x+w]
    roi_color = img[y:y+h, x:x+w]
    eyes = eye_cascade.detectMultiScale(roi_gray)
    for (x_eye,y_eye,w_eye,h_eye) in eyes:
        centers.append((x + int(x_eye + 0.5*w_eye), y +
int(y_eye + 0.5*h_eye)))

if len(centers) > 0:
    # Overlay sunglasses; the factor 2.12 is customizable
depending on the size of the face
    sunglasses_width = 2.12 * abs(centers[1][0] -
centers[0][0])
    overlay_img = np.ones(img.shape, np.uint8) * 255
    h, w = sunglasses_img.shape[:2]
    scaling_factor = sunglasses_width / w
    overlay_sunglasses = cv2.resize(sunglasses_img, None,
fx=scaling_factor,
            fy=scaling_factor, interpolation=cv2.INTER_AREA)

    x = centers[0][0] if centers[0][0] < centers[1][0] else
centers[1][0]

    # customizable X and Y locations; depends on the size of
the face
    x -= 0.26*overlay_sunglasses.shape[1]
    y += 0.85*overlay_sunglasses.shape[0]

    h, w = overlay_sunglasses.shape[:2]
    overlay_img[y:y+h, x:x+w] = overlay_sunglasses

    # Create mask
    gray_sunglasses = cv2.cvtColor(overlay_img,
cv2.COLOR_BGR2GRAY)
    ret, mask = cv2.threshold(gray_sunglasses, 110, 255,
cv2.THRESH_BINARY)
    mask_inv = cv2.bitwise_not(mask)
    temp = cv2.bitwise_and(img, img, mask=mask)
    temp2 = cv2.bitwise_and(overlay_img, overlay_img,
mask=mask_inv)
    final_img = cv2.add(temp, temp2)

    cv2.imshow('Eye Detector', img)
    cv2.imshow('Sunglasses', final_img)
    cv2.waitKey()
    cv2.destroyAllWindows()
```

# Positioning the sunglasses

Just like we did earlier, we load the image and detect the eyes. Once we detect the eyes, we resize the sunglasses image to fit the current region of interest. To create the region of interest, we consider the distance between the eyes. We resize the image accordingly and then go ahead to create a mask. This is similar to what we did with the skull mask earlier. The positioning of the sunglasses on the face is subjective. So you will have to tinker with the weights if you want to use a different pair of sunglasses.

# Detecting ears

Since we know how the pipeline works, let's just jump into the code:

```
import cv2
import numpy as np

left_ear_cascade =
cv2.CascadeClassifier('./cascade_files/haarcascade_mcs_leftear.xml')
right_ear_cascade = cv2.CascadeClassifier('./cascade_files/
haarcascade_mcs_rightear.xml')

if left_ear_cascade.empty():
  raise IOError('Unable to load the left ear cascade
classifier xml file')

if right_ear_cascade.empty():
  raise IOError('Unable to load the right ear cascade classifier xml
file')

img = cv2.imread('input.jpg')

gray = cv2.cvtColor(img, cv2.COLOR_BGR2GRAY)

left_ear = left_ear_cascade.detectMultiScale(gray, 1.3, 5)
right_ear = right_ear_cascade.detectMultiScale(gray, 1.3, 5)

for (x,y,w,h) in left_ear:
    cv2.rectangle(img, (x,y), (x+w,y+h), (0,255,0), 3)

for (x,y,w,h) in right_ear:
    cv2.rectangle(img, (x,y), (x+w,y+h), (255,0,0), 3)

cv2.imshow('Ear Detector', img)
cv2.waitKey()
cv2.destroyAllWindows()
```

If you run the above code on an image, you should see something like the following screenshot:

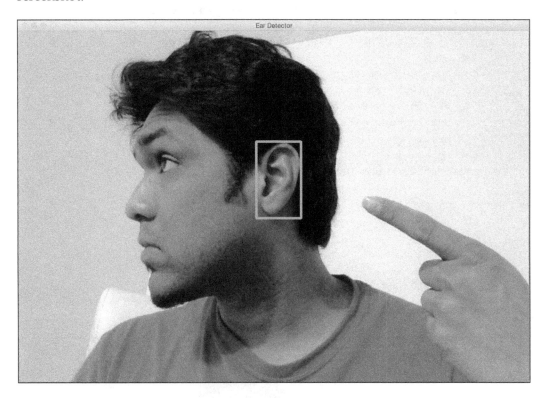

# Detecting a mouth

Following is the code:

```
import cv2
import numpy as np

mouth_cascade =
cv2.CascadeClassifier('./cascade_files/haarcascade_mcs_mouth.xml')

if mouth_cascade.empty():
  raise IOError('Unable to load the mouth cascade classifier
xml file')

cap = cv2.VideoCapture(0)
ds_factor = 0.5
```

```
while True:
    ret, frame = cap.read()
    frame = cv2.resize(frame, None, fx=ds_factor, fy=ds_factor,
interpolation=cv2.INTER_AREA)
    gray = cv2.cvtColor(frame, cv2.COLOR_BGR2GRAY)

    mouth_rects = mouth_cascade.detectMultiScale(gray, 1.7, 11)
    for (x,y,w,h) in mouth_rects:
        y = int(y - 0.15*h)
        cv2.rectangle(frame, (x,y), (x+w,y+h), (0,255,0), 3)
        break

    cv2.imshow('Mouth Detector', frame)

    c = cv2.waitKey(1)
    if c == 27:
        break

cap.release()
cv2.destroyAllWindows()
```

Following is what the output looks like:

# It's time for a moustache

Let's overlay a moustache on top:

```python
import cv2
import numpy as np

mouth_cascade =
cv2.CascadeClassifier('./cascade_files/haarcascade_mcs_mouth.xml')

moustache_mask = cv2.imread('../images/moustache.png')
h_mask, w_mask = moustache_mask.shape[:2]

if mouth_cascade.empty():
  raise IOError('Unable to load the mouth cascade classifier
xml file')

cap = cv2.VideoCapture(0)
scaling_factor = 0.5

while True:
    ret, frame = cap.read()
    frame = cv2.resize(frame, None, fx=scaling_factor,
fy=scaling_factor, interpolation=cv2.INTER_AREA)
    gray = cv2.cvtColor(frame, cv2.COLOR_BGR2GRAY)

    mouth_rects = mouth_cascade.detectMultiScale(gray, 1.3, 5)
    if len(mouth_rects) > 0:
        (x,y,w,h) = mouth_rects[0]
        h, w = int(0.6*h), int(1.2*w)
        x -= 0.05*w
        y -= 0.55*h
        frame_roi = frame[y:y+h, x:x+w]
        moustache_mask_small = cv2.resize(moustache_mask, (w,
h), interpolation=cv2.INTER_AREA)

        gray_mask = cv2.cvtColor(moustache_mask_small,
cv2.COLOR_BGR2GRAY)
        ret, mask = cv2.threshold(gray_mask, 50, 255,
cv2.THRESH_BINARY_INV)
        mask_inv = cv2.bitwise_not(mask)
        masked_mouth = cv2.bitwise_and(moustache_mask_small,
moustache_mask_small, mask=mask)
        masked_frame = cv2.bitwise_and(frame_roi, frame_roi,
mask=mask_inv)
        frame[y:y+h, x:x+w] = cv2.add(masked_mouth,
masked_frame)
```

```
            cv2.imshow('Moustache', frame)

            c = cv2.waitKey(1)
            if c == 27:
                break

    cap.release()
    cv2.destroyAllWindows()
```

Here's what it looks like:

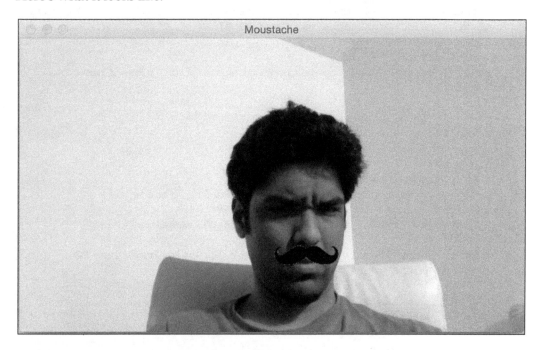

# Detecting a nose

The following program shows how you detect a nose:

```
import cv2
import numpy as np

nose_cascade =
cv2.CascadeClassifier('./cascade_files/haarcascade_mcs_nose.xml')

if nose_cascade.empty():
  raise IOError('Unable to load the nose cascade classifier
xml file')
```

```python
cap = cv2.VideoCapture(0)
ds_factor = 0.5

while True:
    ret, frame = cap.read()
    frame = cv2.resize(frame, None, fx=ds_factor, fy=ds_factor,
interpolation=cv2.INTER_AREA)
    gray = cv2.cvtColor(frame, cv2.COLOR_BGR2GRAY)

    nose_rects = nose_cascade.detectMultiScale(gray, 1.3, 5)
    for (x,y,w,h) in nose_rects:
        cv2.rectangle(frame, (x,y), (x+w,y+h), (0,255,0), 3)
        break

    cv2.imshow('Nose Detector', frame)

    c = cv2.waitKey(1)
    if c == 27:
        break

cap.release()
cv2.destroyAllWindows()
```

The output looks something like the following image:

# Detecting pupils

We are going to take a different approach here. Pupils are too generic to take the Haar cascade approach. We will also get a sense of how to detect things based on their shape. Following is what the output will look like:

Let's see how to build the pupil detector:

```
import math

import cv2
import numpy as np

img = cv2.imread('input.jpg')
scaling_factor = 0.7

img = cv2.resize(img, None, fx=scaling_factor,
fy=scaling_factor, interpolation=cv2.INTER_AREA)
cv2.imshow('Input', img)
gray = cv2.cvtColor(~img, cv2.COLOR_BGR2GRAY)
```

```
ret, thresh_gray = cv2.threshold(gray, 220, 255,
cv2.THRESH_BINARY)
contours, hierarchy = cv2.findContours(thresh_gray,
cv2.RETR_EXTERNAL, cv2.CHAIN_APPROX_NONE)

for contour in contours:
    area = cv2.contourArea(contour)
    rect = cv2.boundingRect(contour)
    x, y, width, height = rect
    radius = 0.25 * (width + height)

    area_condition = (100 <= area <= 200)
    symmetry_condition = (abs(1 - float(width)/float(height))
<= 0.2)
    fill_condition = (abs(1 - (area / (math.pi * math.pow(radius,
2.0)))) <= 0.3)

    if area_condition and symmetry_condition and fill_condition:
        cv2.circle(img, (int(x + radius), int(y + radius)),
int(1.3*radius), (0,180,0), -1)

cv2.imshow('Pupil Detector', img)

c = cv2.waitKey()
cv2.destroyAllWindows()
```

If you run this program, you will see the output as shown earlier.

# Deconstructing the code

As we discussed earlier, we are not going to use Haar cascade to detect pupils. If we can't use a pre-trained classifier, then how are we going to detect the pupils? Well, we can use shape analysis to detect the pupils. We know that pupils are circular, so we can use this information to detect them in the image. We invert the input image and then convert it into grayscale image as shown in the following line:

```
gray = cv2.cvtColor(~img, cv2.COLOR_BGR2GRAY)
```

As we can see here, we can invert an image using the tilde operator. Inverting the image is helpful in our case because the pupil is black in color, and black corresponds to a low pixel value. We then threshold the image to make sure that there are only black and white pixels. Now, we have to find out the boundaries of all the shapes. OpenCV provides a nice function to achieve this, that is findContours. We will discuss more about this in the upcoming chapters. But for now, all we need to know is that this function returns the set of boundaries of all the shapes that are found in the image.

The next step is to identify the shape of the pupil and discard the rest. We will use certain properties of the circle to zero-in on this shape. Let's consider the ratio of width to height of the bounding rectangle. If the shape is a circle, this ratio will be 1. We can use the function `boundingRect` to obtain the coordinates of the bounding rectangle. Let's consider the area of this shape. If we roughly compute the radius of this shape and use the formula for the area of the circle, then it should be close to the area of this contour. We can use the function `contourArea` to compute the area of any contour in the image. So we can use these conditions and filter out the shapes. After we do that, we are left with two pupils in the image. We can refine it further by limiting the search region to the face or the eyes. Since you know how to detect faces and eyes, you can give it a try and see if you can get it working for a live video stream.

# Summary

In this chapter, we discussed Haar cascades and integral images. We understood how the face detection pipeline is built. We learnt how to detect and track faces in a live video stream. We discussed how to use the face detection pipeline to detect various body parts like eyes, ears, nose, and mouth. We learnt how to overlay masks on top on the input image using the results of body parts detection. We used the principles of shape analysis to detect the pupils.

In the next chapter, we are going to discuss feature detection and how it can be used to understand the image content.

# 5

# Extracting Features from an Image

In this chapter, we are going to learn how to detect salient points, also known as keypoints, in an image. We will discuss why these keypoints are important and how we can use them to understand the image content. We will talk about different techniques that can be used to detect these keypoints, and understand how we can extract features from a given image.

By the end of this chapter, you will know:

- What are keypoints and why do we care about them
- How to detect keypoints
- How to use keypoints for image content analysis
- The different techniques to detect keypoints
- How to build a feature extractor

## Why do we care about keypoints?

Image content analysis refers to the process of understanding the content of an image so that we can take some action based on that. Let's take a step back and talk about how humans do it. Our brain is an extremely powerful machine that can do complicated things very quickly. When we look at something, our brain automatically creates a footprint based on the "interesting" aspects of that image. We will discuss what interesting means as we move along this chapter.

For now, an interesting aspect is something that's distinct in that region. If we call a point interesting, then there shouldn't be another point in its neighborhood that satisfies the constraints. Let's consider the following image:

Now close your eyes and try to visualize this image. Do you see something specific? Can you recollect what's in the left half of the image? Not really! The reason for this is that the image doesn't have any interesting information. When our brain looks at something like this, there's nothing to make note of. So it tends to wander around! Let's take a look at the following image:

Now close your eyes and try to visualize this image. You will see that the recollection is vivid and you remember a lot of details about this image. The reason for this is that there are a lot of interesting regions in the image. The human eye is more sensitive to high frequency content as compared to low frequency content. This is the reason we tend to recollect the second image better than the first one. To further demonstrate this, let's look at the following image:

If you notice, your eye immediately went to the TV remote, even though it's not at the center of the image. We automatically tend to gravitate towards the interesting regions in the image because that is where all the information is. This is what our brain needs to store in order to recollect it later.

When we build object recognition systems, we need to detect these "interesting" regions to create a signature for the image. These interesting regions are characterized by keypoints. This is why keypoint detection is critical in many modern computer vision systems.

# What are keypoints?

Now that we know that keypoints refer to the interesting regions in the image, let's dig a little deeper. What are keypoints made of? Where are these points? When we say "interesting", it means that something is happening in that region. If the region is just uniform, then it's not very interesting. For example, corners are interesting because there is sharp change in intensity in two different directions. Each corner is a unique point where two edges meet. If you look at the preceding images, you will see that the interesting regions are not completely made up of "interesting" content. If you look closely, we can still see plain regions within busy regions. For example, consider the following image:

If you look at the preceding object, the interior parts of the interesting regions are "uninteresting".

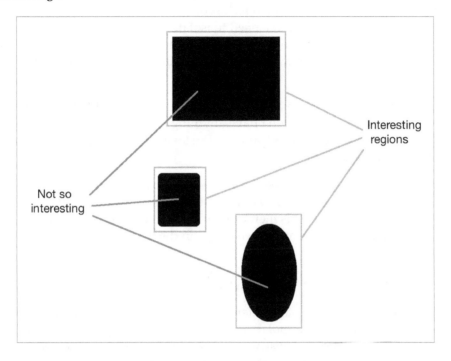

So, if we were to characterize this object, we would need to make sure that we picked the interesting points. Now, how do we define "interesting points"? Can we just say that anything that's not uninteresting can be an interesting point? Let's consider the following example:

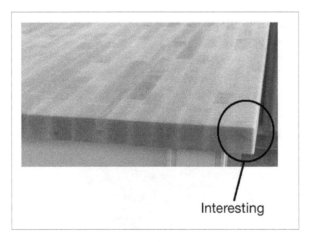

Now, we can see that there is a lot of high frequency content in this image along the edge. But we cannot call the whole edge "interesting". It is important to understand that "interesting" doesn't necessarily refer to color or intensity values. It can be anything, as long as it is distinct. We need to isolate the points that are unique in their neighborhood. The points along the edge are not unique with respect to their neighbors. So, now that we know what we are looking for, how do we pick an interesting point?

What about the corner of the table? That's pretty interesting, right? It's unique with respect to its neighbors and we don't have anything like that in its vicinity. Now this point can be chosen as one of our keypoints. We take a bunch of these keypoints to characterize a particular image.

When we do image analysis, we need to convert it into a numerical form before we deduce something. These keypoints are represented using a numerical form and a combination of these keypoints is then used to create the image signature. We want this image signature to represent a given image in the best possible way.

# Detecting the corners

Since we know that the corners are "interesting", let's see how we can detect them. In computer vision, there is a popular corner detection technique called **Harris Corner Detector**. We basically construct a 2x2 matrix based on partial derivatives of the grayscale image, and then analyze the eigenvalues. This is actually an oversimplification of the actual algorithm, but it covers the gist. So, if you want to understand the underlying mathematical details, you can look into the original paper by Harris and Stephens at http://www.bmva.org/bmvc/1988/avc-88-023.pdf. A corner point is a point where both the eigenvalues would have large values.

Let's consider the following image:

If you run the Harris corner detector on this image, you will see something like this:

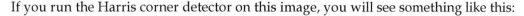
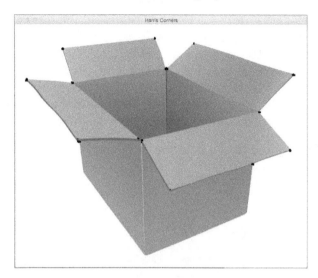

As you can see, all the black dots correspond to the corners in the image. If you notice, the corners at the bottom of the box are not detected. The reason for this is that the corners are not sharp enough. You can adjust the thresholds in the corner detector to identify these corners. The code to do this is as follows:

```
import cv2
import numpy as np

img = cv2.imread('box.jpg')
gray = cv2.cvtColor(img,cv2.COLOR_BGR2GRAY)

gray = np.float32(gray)

dst = cv2.cornerHarris(gray, 4,5, 0.04)        # to detect only
sharp corners
#dst = cv2.cornerHarris(gray, 14, 5, 0.04)     # to detect soft
corners

# Result is dilated for marking the corners
dst = cv2.dilate(dst,None)

# Threshold for an optimal value, it may vary depending on the
image.
img[dst > 0.01*dst.max()] = [0,0,0]

cv2.imshow('Harris Corners',img)
cv2.waitKey()
```

# Good Features To Track

Harris corner detector performs well in many cases, but it misses out on a few things. Around six years after the original paper by Harris and Stephens, Shi-Tomasi came up with a better corner detector. You can read the original paper at http://www. ai.mit.edu/courses/6.891/handouts/shi94good.pdf. They used a different scoring function to improve the overall quality. Using this method, we can find the 'N' strongest corners in the given image. This is very useful when we don't want to use every single corner to extract information from the image.

If you apply the Shi-Tomasi corner detector to the image shown earlier, you will see something like this:

Following is the code:

```
import cv2
import numpy as np

img = cv2.imread('box.jpg')
gray = cv2.cvtColor(img,cv2.COLOR_BGR2GRAY)

corners = cv2.goodFeaturesToTrack(gray, 7, 0.05, 25)
corners = np.float32(corners)
```

```
for item in corners:
    x, y = item[0]
    cv2.circle(img, (x,y), 5, 255, -1)

cv2.imshow("Top 'k' features", img)
cv2.waitKey()
```

# Scale Invariant Feature Transform (SIFT)

Even though corner features are "interesting", they are not good enough to characterize the truly interesting parts. When we talk about image content analysis, we want the image signature to be invariant to things such as scale, rotation, illumination, and so on. Humans are very good at these things. Even if I show you an image of an apple upside down that's dimmed, you will still recognize it. If I show you a really enlarged version of that image, you will still recognize it. We want our image recognition systems to be able to do the same.

Let's consider the corner features. If you enlarge an image, a corner might stop being a corner as shown below.

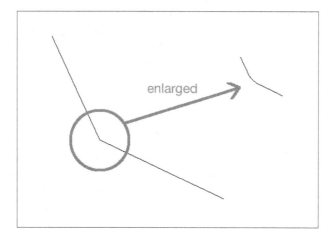

In the second case, the detector will not pick up this corner. And, since it was picked up in the original image, the second image will not be matched with the first one. It's basically the same image, but the corner features based method will totally miss it. This means that corner detector is not exactly scale invariant. This is why we need a better method to characterize an image.

SIFT is one of the most popular algorithms in all of computer vision. You can read David Lowe's original paper at `http://www.cs.ubc.ca/~lowe/papers/ijcv04.pdf`. We can use this algorithm to extract keypoints and build the corresponding feature descriptors. There is a lot of good documentation available online, so we will keep our discussion brief. To identify a potential keypoint, SIFT builds a pyramid by downsampling an image and taking the difference of Gaussian. This means that we run a Gaussian filter at each level and take the difference to build the successive levels in the pyramid. In order to see if the current point is a keypoint, it looks at the neighbors as well as the pixels at the same location in neighboring levels of the pyramid. If it's a maxima, then the current point is picked up as a keypoint. This ensures that we keep the keypoints scale invariant.

Now that we know how it achieves scale invariance, let's see how it achieves rotation invariance. Once we identify the keypoints, each keypoint is assigned an orientation. We take the neighborhood around each keypoint and compute the gradient magnitude and direction. This gives us a sense of the direction of that keypoint. If we have this information, we will be able to match this keypoint to the same point in another image even if it's rotated. Since we know the orientation, we will be able to normalize those keypoints before making the comparisons.

Once we have all this information, how do we quantify it? We need to convert it to a set of numbers so that we can do some kind of matching on it. To achieve this, we just take the 16x16 neighborhood around each keypoint, and divide it into 16 blocks of size 4x4. For each block, we compute the orientation histogram with 8 bins. So, we have a vector of length 8 associated with each block, which means that the neighborhood is represented by a vector of size 128 (8x16). This is the final keypoint descriptor that will be used. If we extract N keypoints from an image, then we will have N descriptors of length 128 each. This array of N descriptors characterizes the given image.

Consider the following image:

If you extract the keypoint locations using SIFT, you will see something like the following, where the size of the circle indicates the strength of the keypoints, and the line inside the circle indicates the orientation:

Before we look at the code, it is important to know that SIFT is patented and it's not freely available for commercial use. Following is the code to do it:

```
import cv2
import numpy as np

input_image = cv2.imread('input.jpg')
gray_image = cv2.cvtColor(input_image, cv2.COLOR_BGR2GRAY)

sift = cv2.SIFT()
keypoints = sift.detect(gray_image, None)

input_image = cv2.drawKeypoints(input_image, keypoints,
flags=cv2.DRAW_MATCHES_FLAGS_DRAW_RICH_KEYPOINTS)

cv2.imshow('SIFT features', input_image)
cv2.waitKey()
```

We can also compute the descriptors. OpenCV lets us do it separately or we can combine the detection and computation parts in the same step by using the following:

```
keypoints, descriptors = sift.detectAndCompute(gray_image,
None)
```

# Speeded Up Robust Features (SURF)

Even though SIFT is nice and useful, it's computationally intensive. This means that it's slow and we will have a hard time implementing a real-time system if it uses SIFT. We need a system that's fast and has all the advantages of SIFT. If you remember, SIFT uses the difference of Gaussian to build the pyramid and this process is slow. So, to overcome this, SURF uses a simple box filter to approximate the Gaussian. The good thing is that this is really easy to compute and it's reasonably fast. There's a lot of documentation available online on SURF at http://opencv-python-tutroals.readthedocs.org/en/latest/py_tutorials/py_feature2d/py_surf_intro/py_surf_intro.html?highlight=surf. So, you can go through it to see how they construct a descriptor. You can refer to the original paper at http://www.vision.ee.ethz.ch/~surf/eccv06.pdf. It is important to know that SURF is also patented and it is not freely available for commercial use.

If you run the SURF keypoint detector on the earlier image, you will see something like the following one:

Here is the code:

```
import cv2
import numpy as np

img = cv2.imread('input.jpg')
gray= cv2.cvtColor(img, cv2.COLOR_BGR2GRAY)

surf = cv2.SURF()

# This threshold controls the number of keypoints
surf.hessianThreshold = 15000

kp, des = surf.detectAndCompute(gray, None)

img = cv2.drawKeypoints(img, kp, None, (0,255,0), 4)

cv2.imshow('SURF features', img)
cv2.waitKey()
```

# Features from Accelerated Segment Test (FAST)

Even though SURF is faster than SIFT, it's just not fast enough for a real-time system, especially when there are resource constraints. When you are building a real-time application on a mobile device, you won't have the luxury of using SURF to do computations in real time. We need something that's really fast and computationally inexpensive. Hence, Rosten and Drummond came up with FAST. As the name indicates, it's really fast!

Instead of going through all the expensive calculations, they came up with a high-speed test to quickly determine if the current point is a potential keypoint. We need to note that FAST is just for keypoint detection. Once keypoints are detected, we need to use SIFT or SURF to compute the descriptors. Consider the following image:

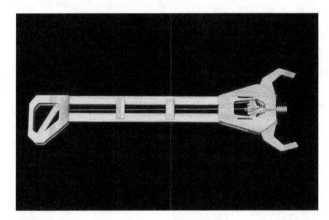

If we run the FAST keypoint detector on this image, you will see something like this:

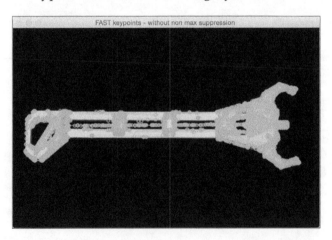

If we clean it up and suppress the unimportant keypoints, it will look like this:

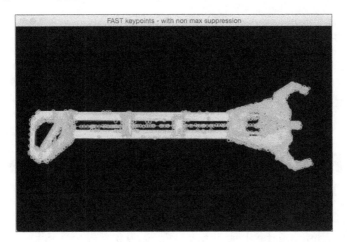

Following is the code for this:

```
import cv2
import numpy as np

gray_image = cv2.imread('input.jpg', 0)

fast = cv2.FastFeatureDetector()

# Detect keypoints
keypoints = fast.detect(gray_image, None)
print "Number of keypoints with non max suppression:",
len(keypoints)

# Draw keypoints on top of the input image
img_keypoints_with_nonmax = cv2.drawKeypoints(gray_image,
keypoints, color=(0,255,0))
cv2.imshow('FAST keypoints - with non max suppression',
img_keypoints_with_nonmax)

# Disable nonmaxSuppression
fast.setBool('nonmaxSuppression', False)

# Detect keypoints again
keypoints = fast.detect(gray_image, None)
```

```
print "Total Keypoints without nonmaxSuppression:",
len(keypoints)

# Draw keypoints on top of the input image
img_keypoints_without_nonmax = cv2.drawKeypoints(gray_image,
keypoints, color=(0,255,0))
cv2.imshow('FAST keypoints - without non max suppression',
img_keypoints_without_nonmax)
cv2.waitKey()
```

# Binary Robust Independent Elementary Features (BRIEF)

Even though we have FAST to quickly detect the keypoints, we still have to use SIFT or SURF to compute the descriptors. We need a way to quickly compute the descriptors as well. This is where BRIEF comes into the picture. BRIEF is a method for extracting feature descriptors. It cannot detect the keypoints by itself, so we need to use it in conjunction with a keypoint detector. The good thing about BRIEF is that it's compact and fast.

Consider the following image:

BRIEF takes the list of input keypoints and outputs an updated list. So if you run BRIEF on this image, you will see something like this:

Following is the code:

```
import cv2
import numpy as np

gray_image = cv2.imread('input.jpg', 0)

# Initiate FAST detector
fast = cv2.FastFeatureDetector()

# Initiate BRIEF extractor
brief = cv2.DescriptorExtractor_create("BRIEF")
```

```
# find the keypoints with STAR
keypoints = fast.detect(gray_image, None)

# compute the descriptors with BRIEF
keypoints, descriptors = brief.compute(gray_image, keypoints)

gray_keypoints = cv2.drawKeypoints(gray_image, keypoints,
color=(0,255,0))
cv2.imshow('BRIEF keypoints', gray_keypoints)
cv2.waitKey()
```

# Oriented FAST and Rotated BRIEF (ORB)

So, now we have arrived at the best combination out of all the combinations that we have discussed so far. This algorithm came out of the OpenCV Labs. It's fast, robust, and open-source! Both SIFT and SURF algorithms are patented and you can't use them for commercial purposes. This is why ORB is good in many ways.

If you run the ORB keypoint extractor on one of the images shown earlier, you will see something like the following:

Here is the code:

```
import cv2
import numpy as np

input_image = cv2.imread('input.jpg')
gray_image = cv2.cvtColor(input_image, cv2.COLOR_BGR2GRAY)

# Initiate ORB object
orb = cv2.ORB()

# find the keypoints with ORB
keypoints = orb.detect(gray_image, None)

# compute the descriptors with ORB
keypoints, descriptors = orb.compute(gray_image, keypoints)

# draw only the location of the keypoints without size or
orientation
final_keypoints = cv2.drawKeypoints(input_image, keypoints,
color=(0,255,0), flags=0)

cv2.imshow('ORB keypoints', final_keypoints)
cv2.waitKey()
```

# Summary

In this chapter, we learned about the importance of keypoints and why we need them. We discussed various algorithms to detect keypoints and compute feature descriptors. We will be using these algorithms in all the subsequent chapters in various different contexts. The concept of keypoints is central to computer vision, and plays an important role in many modern systems.

In the next chapter, we are going to discuss how to stitch multiple images of the same scene together to create a panoramic image.

# 6
# Creating a Panoramic Image

In this chapter, we are going to learn how to stitch multiple images of the same scene together to create a panoramic image.

By the end of this chapter, you will know:

- How to match keypoint descriptors between multiple images
- How to find overlapping regions between images
- How to warp images based on the matching keypoints
- How to stitch multiple images to create a panoramic image

## Matching keypoint descriptors

In the last chapter, we learned how to extract keypoints using various methods. The reason that we extract keypoints is because we can use them for image matching. Let's consider the following image:

As you can see, it's the picture of a school bus. Now, let's take a look at the following image:

The preceding image is a part of the school bus image and it's been rotated anticlockwise by 90 degrees. We could easily recognize this because our brain is invariant to scaling and rotation. Our goal here is to find the matching points between these two images. If you do that, it would look something like this:

Following is the code to do this:

```
import sys

import cv2
import numpy as np

def draw_matches(img1, keypoints1, img2, keypoints2, matches):
    rows1, cols1 = img1.shape[:2]
    rows2, cols2 = img2.shape[:2]

    # Create a new output image that concatenates the two images
together
    output_img = np.zeros((max([rows1,rows2]), cols1+cols2, 3),
dtype='uint8')
    output_img[:rows1, :cols1, :] = np.dstack([img1, img1, img1])
    output_img[:rows2, cols1:cols1+cols2, :] = np.dstack([img2, img2,
img2])

    # Draw connecting lines between matching keypoints
    for match in matches:
        # Get the matching keypoints for each of the images
        img1_idx = match.queryIdx
        img2_idx = match.trainIdx

        (x1, y1) = keypoints1[img1_idx].pt
        (x2, y2) = keypoints2[img2_idx].pt

        # Draw a small circle at both co-ordinates and then draw a
line
        radius = 4
        colour = (0,255,0)    # green
        thickness = 1
        cv2.circle(output_img, (int(x1),int(y1)), radius, colour,
thickness)
        cv2.circle(output_img, (int(x2)+cols1,int(y2)), radius,
colour, thickness)
        cv2.line(output_img, (int(x1),int(y1)),
(int(x2)+cols1,int(y2)), colour, thickness)

    return output_img

if __name__=='__main__':
    img1 = cv2.imread(sys.argv[1], 0)    # query image (rotated
subregion)
```

```
    img2 = cv2.imread(sys.argv[2], 0)    # train image (full image)

    # Initialize ORB detector
    orb = cv2.ORB()

    # Extract keypoints and descriptors
    keypoints1, descriptors1 = orb.detectAndCompute(img1, None)
    keypoints2, descriptors2 = orb.detectAndCompute(img2, None)

    # Create Brute Force matcher object
    bf = cv2.BFMatcher(cv2.NORM_HAMMING, crossCheck=True)

    # Match descriptors
    matches = bf.match(descriptors1, descriptors2)

    # Sort them in the order of their distance
    matches = sorted(matches, key = lambda x:x.distance)

    # Draw first 'n' matches
    img3 = draw_matches(img1, keypoints1, img2, keypoints2,
matches[:30])

    cv2.imshow('Matched keypoints', img3)
    cv2.waitKey()
```

# How did we match the keypoints?

In the preceding code, we used the ORB detector to extract the keypoints. Once we extracted the keypoints, we used the Brute Force matcher to match the descriptors. Brute Force matching is pretty straightforward! For every descriptor in the first image, we match it with every descriptor in the second image and take the closest one. To compute the closest descriptor, we use the Hamming distance as the metric, as shown in the following line:

```
    bf = cv2.BFMatcher(cv2.NORM_HAMMING, crossCheck=True)
```

You can read more about the Hamming distance at https://en.wikipedia.org/wiki/Hamming_distance. The second argument in the preceding line is a Boolean variable. If this is true, then the matcher returns only those keypoints that are closest to each other in both directions. This means that if we get (i, j) as a match, then we can be sure that the i-th descriptor in the first image has the j-th descriptor in the second image as its closest match and vice versa. This increases the consistency and robustness of descriptor matching.

# Understanding the matcher object

Let's consider the following line again:

```
matches = bf.match(descriptors1, descriptors2)
```

Here, the variable matches is a list of DMatch objects. You can read more about it in the OpenCV documentation. We just need to quickly understand what it means because it will become increasingly relevant in the upcoming chapters. If we are iterating over this list of DMatch objects, then each item will have the following attributes:

- **item.distance**: This attribute gives us the distance between the descriptors. A lower distance indicates a better match.

- **item.trainIdx**: This attribute gives us the index of the descriptor in the list of train descriptors (in our case, it's the list of descriptors in the full image).

- **item.queryIdx**: This attribute gives us the index of the descriptor in the list of query descriptors (in our case, it's the list of descriptors in the rotated subimage).

- **item.imgIdx**: This attribute gives us the index of the train image.

# Drawing the matching keypoints

Now that we know how to access different attributes of the matcher object, let's see how we can use them to draw the matching keypoints. OpenCV 3.0 provides a direct function to draw the matching keypoints, but we will not be using that. It's better to take a peek inside to see what's happening underneath.

We need to create a big output image that can fit both the images side by side. So, we do that in the following line:

```
output_img = np.zeros((max([rows1,rows2]), cols1+cols2, 3),
dtype='uint8')
```

As we can see here, the number of rows is set to the bigger of the two values and the number of columns is simply the sum of both the values. For each item in the list of matches, we extract the locations of the matching keypoints, as we can see in the following lines:

```
(x1, y1) = keypoints1[img1_idx].pt
(x2, y2) = keypoints2[img2_idx].pt
```

Once we do that, we just draw circles on those points to indicate their locations and then draw a line connecting the two points.

# Creating the panoramic image

Now that we know how to match keypoints, let's go ahead and see how we can stitch multiple images together. Consider the following image:

Let's say we want to stitch the following image with the preceding image:

If we stitch these images, it will look something like the following one:

Now let's say we captured another part of this house, as seen in the following image:

If we stitch the preceding image with the stitched image we saw earlier, it will look something like this:

We can keep stitching images together to create a nice panoramic image. Let's take a look at the code:

```
import sys
import argparse

import cv2
import numpy as np

def argument_parser():
    parser = argparse.ArgumentParser(description='Stitch two
images together')
    parser.add_argument("--query-image", dest="query_image",
required=True,
            help="First image that needs to be stitched")
    parser.add_argument("--train-image", dest="train_image",
required=True,
            help="Second image that needs to be stitched")
    parser.add_argument("--min-match-count",
dest="min_match_count", type=int,
            required=False, default=10, help="Minimum number of
matches required")
    return parser
```

```
# Warp img2 to img1 using the homography matrix H
def warpImages(img1, img2, H):
    rows1, cols1 = img1.shape[:2]
    rows2, cols2 = img2.shape[:2]

    list_of_points_1 = np.float32([[0,0], [0,rows1],
[cols1,rows1], [cols1,0]]).reshape(-1,1,2)
    temp_points = np.float32([[0,0], [0,rows2], [cols2,rows2],
[cols2,0]]).reshape(-1,1,2)
    list_of_points_2 = cv2.perspectiveTransform(temp_points, H)
    list_of_points = np.concatenate((list_of_points_1,
list_of_points_2), axis=0)

    [x_min, y_min] = np.int32(list_of_points.min(axis=0).ravel() -
0.5)
    [x_max, y_max] = np.int32(list_of_points.max(axis=0).ravel() +
0.5)
    translation_dist = [-x_min,-y_min]
    H_translation = np.array([[1, 0, translation_dist[0]], [0, 1,
translation_dist[1]], [0,0,1]])

    output_img = cv2.warpPerspective(img2, H_translation.dot(H),
(x_max-x_min, y_max-y_min))
    output_img[translation_dist[1]:rows1+translation_dist[1],
translation_dist[0]:cols1+translation_dist[0]] = img1

    return output_img

if __name__=='__main__':
    args = argument_parser().parse_args()
    img1 = cv2.imread(args.query_image, 0)
    img2 = cv2.imread(args.train_image, 0)
    min_match_count = args.min_match_count

    cv2.imshow('Query image', img1)
    cv2.imshow('Train image', img2)

    # Initialize the SIFT detector
    sift = cv2.SIFT()

    # Extract the keypoints and descriptors
    keypoints1, descriptors1 = sift.detectAndCompute(img1, None)
    keypoints2, descriptors2 = sift.detectAndCompute(img2, None)
```

```
# Initialize parameters for Flann based matcher
FLANN_INDEX_KDTREE = 0
index_params = dict(algorithm = FLANN_INDEX_KDTREE, trees = 5)
search_params = dict(checks = 50)

# Initialize the Flann based matcher object
flann = cv2.FlannBasedMatcher(index_params, search_params)

# Compute the matches
matches = flann.knnMatch(descriptors1, descriptors2, k=2)

# Store all the good matches as per Lowe's ratio test
good_matches = []
for m1,m2 in matches:
    if m1.distance < 0.7*m2.distance:
        good_matches.append(m1)

if len(good_matches) > min_match_count:
    src_pts = np.float32([ keypoints1[good_match.queryIdx].pt
for good_match in good_matches ]).reshape(-1,1,2)
    dst_pts = np.float32([ keypoints2[good_match.trainIdx].pt
for good_match in good_matches ]).reshape(-1,1,2)

    M, mask = cv2.findHomography(src_pts, dst_pts, cv2.RANSAC,
5.0)
    result = warpImages(img2, img1, M)
    cv2.imshow('Stitched output', result)

    cv2.waitKey()

else:
    print "We don't have enough number of matches between the
two images."
    print "Found only %d matches. We need at least %d
matches." % (len(good_matches), min_match_count)
```

# Finding the overlapping regions

The goal here is to find the matching keypoints so that we can stitch the images
together. So, the first step is to get these matching keypoints. As discussed in the
previous section, we use a keypoint detector to extract the keypoints, and then
use a Flann based matcher to match the keypoints.

You can learn more about Flann at `http://citeseerx.ist.psu.edu/viewdoc/download?doi=10.1.1.192.5378&rep=rep1&type=pdf`.

The Flann based matcher is faster than Brute Force matching because it doesn't compare each point with every single point on the other list. It only considers the neighborhood of the current point to get the matching keypoint, thereby making it more efficient.

Once we get a list of matching keypoints, we use Lowe's ratio test to keep only the strong matches. David Lowe proposed this ratio test in order to increase the robustness of SIFT.

 You can read more about this at `http://www.cs.ubc.ca/~lowe/papers/ijcv04.pdf`.

Basically, when we match the keypoints, we reject the matches in which the ratio of the distances to the nearest neighbor and the second nearest neighbor is greater than a certain threshold. This helps us in discarding the points that are not distinct enough. So, we use that concept here to keep only the good matches and discard the rest. If we don't have sufficient matches, we don't proceed further. In our case, the default value is 10. You can play around with this input parameter to see how it affects the output.

If we have a sufficient number of matches, then we extract the list of keypoints in both the images and extract the homography matrix. If you remember, we have already discussed homography in the first chapter. So if you have forgotten about it, you may want to take a quick look. We basically take a bunch of points from both the images and extract the transformation matrix.

# Stitching the images

Now that we have the transformation, we can go ahead and stitch the images. We will use the transformation matrix to transform the second list of points. We keep the first image as the frame of reference and create an output image that's big enough to hold both the images. We need to extract information about the transformation of the second image. We need to move it into this frame of reference to make sure it aligns with the first image. So, we have to extract the translation information and then warp it. We then add the first image into this and construct the final output. It is worth mentioning that this works for images with different aspect ratios as well. So, if you get a chance, try it out and see what the output looks like.

# What if the images are at an angle to each other?

Until now, we were looking at images that were on the same plane. Stitching those images was straightforward and we didn't have to deal with any artifacts. In real life, you cannot capture multiple images on exactly the same plane. When you are capturing multiple images of the same scene, you are bound to tilt your camera and change the plane. So the question is, will our algorithm work in that scenario? As it turns out, it can handle those cases as well.

Let's consider the following image:

Now, let's consider another image of the same scene. It's at an angle with respect to the first image, and it's partially overlapping as well:

Let's consider the first image as our reference. If we stitch these images using our algorithm, it will look something like this:

If we keep the second image as our reference, it will look something like this:

## Why does it look stretched?

If you observe, a portion of the output image corresponding to the query image looks stretched. It's because the query image is transformed and adjusted to fit into our frame of reference. The reason it looks stretched is because of the following lines in our code:

```
M, mask = cv2.findHomography(src_pts, dst_pts, cv2.RANSAC, 5.0)
result = warpImages(img2, img1, M)
```

Since the images are at an angle with respect to each other, the query image will have to undergo a perspective transformation in order to fit into the frame of reference. So, we transform the query image first, and then stitch it into our main image to form the panoramic image.

## Summary

In this chapter, we learned how to match keypoints among multiple images. We discussed how to stitch multiple images together to create a panoramic image. We learned how to deal with images that are not on the same plane.

In the next chapter, we are going to discuss how to do content-aware image resizing by detecting "interesting" regions in the image.

# 7
# Seam Carving

In this chapter, we are going to learn about content-aware image resizing, which is also known as seam carving. We will discuss how to detect "interesting" parts in an image and how to use that information to resize a given image without deteriorating those interesting parts.

By the end of this chapter, you will know:

- What is content awareness
- How to quantify "interesting" parts in an image
- How to use dynamic programming for image content analysis
- How to increase and decrease the width of an image without deteriorating the interesting regions while keeping the height constant
- How to make an object disappear from an image

# Why do we care about seam carving?

Before we start our discussion about seam carving, we need to understand why it is needed in the first place. Why should we care about the image content? Why can't we just resize the given image and move on with our lives? Well, to answer that question, let's consider the following image:

Now, let's say we want to reduce the width of this image while keeping the height constant. If you do that, it will look something like this:

As you can see, the ducks in the image look skewed, and there's degradation in the overall quality of the image. Intuitively speaking, we can say that the ducks are the "interesting" parts in the image. So when we resize it, we want the ducks to be intact. This is where seam carving comes into the picture. Using seam carving, we can detect these interesting regions and make sure they don't get degraded.

# How does it work?

We have been talking about image resizing and how we should consider the image's content when we resize it. So, why on earth is it called seam carving? It should just be called content-aware image resizing, right? Well, there are many different terms that are used to describe this process, such as image retargeting, liquid scaling, seam carving, and so on. The reason it's called seam carving is because of the way we resize the image. The algorithm was proposed by Shai Avidan and Ariel Shamir. You can refer to the original paper at http://dl.acm.org/citation.cfm?id=1276390.

We know that the goal is to resize the given image and keep the interesting content intact. So, we do that by finding the paths of least importance in that image. These paths are called seams. Once we find these seams, we remove them from the image to obtain a rescaled image. This process of removing, or "carving", will eventually result in a resized image. This is the reason we call it "seam carving". Consider the image that follows:

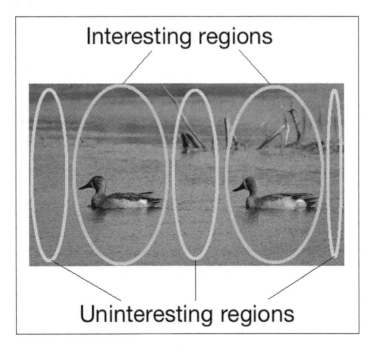

In the preceding image, we can see how we can roughly divide the image into interesting and uninteresting parts. We need to make sure that our algorithm detects these uninteresting parts and removes them. Let's consider the ducks image and the constraints we have to work with. We need to keep the height constant. This means that we need to find vertical seams in the image and remove them. These seams start at the top and end at the bottom (or vice versa). If we were dealing with vertical resizing, then the seams would start on the left-hand side and end on the right. A vertical seam is just a bunch of connected pixels starting at the top row and ending at the last row in the image.

# How do we define "interesting"?

Before we start computing the seams, we need to find out what metric we will be using to compute these seams. We need a way to assign "importance" to each pixel so that we can find out the paths that are least important. In computer vision terminology, we say that we need to assign an energy value to each pixel so that we can find the path of minimum energy. Coming up with a good way to assign the energy value is very important because it will affect the quality of the output.

One of the metrics that we can use is the value of the derivative at each point. This is a good indicator of the level of activity in that neighborhood. If there is some activity, then the pixel values will change rapidly. Hence the value of the derivative at that point would be high. On the other hand, if the region were plain and uninteresting, then the pixel values wouldn't change as rapidly. So, the value of the derivative at that point in the grayscale image would be low.

For each pixel location, we compute the energy by summing up the X and Y derivatives at that point. We compute the derivatives by taking the difference between the current pixel and its neighbors. If you recall, we did something similar to this when we were doing edge detection using **Sobel Filter** in *Chapter 2*, *Detecting Edges and Applying Image Filters*. Once we compute these values, we store them in a matrix called the energy matrix.

# How do we compute the seams?

Now that we have the energy matrix, we are ready to compute the seams. We need to find the path through the image with the least energy. Computing all the possible paths is prohibitively expensive, so we need to find a smarter way to do this. This is where dynamic programming comes into the picture. In fact, seam carving is a direct application of dynamic programming. We need to start with each pixel in the first row and find our way to the last row. In order to find the path of least energy, we compute and store the best paths to each pixel in a table. Once we've construct this table, the path to a particular pixel can be found by backtracking through the rows in that table.

For each pixel in the current row, we calculate the energy of three possible pixel locations in the next row that we can move to, that is, bottom left, bottom, and bottom right. We keep repeating this process until we reach the bottom. Once we reach the bottom, we take the one with the least cumulative value and backtrack our way to the top. This will give us the path of least energy. Every time we remove a seam, the width of the image decreases by 1. So we need to keep removing these seams until we arrive at the required image size.

Let's consider our ducks image again. If you compute the first 30 seams, it will look something like this:

These green lines indicate the paths of least importance. As we can see here, they carefully go around the ducks to make sure that the interesting regions are not touched. In the upper half of the image, the seams go around the twigs so that the quality is preserved. Technically speaking, the twigs are also "interesting". If you continue and remove the first 100 seams, it will look something like this:

Now, compare this with the naively resized image. Doesn't it look much better? The ducks look nice in this image.

Let's take a look at the code and see how to do it:

```
import sys

import cv2
import numpy as np

# Draw vertical seam on top of the image
def overlay_vertical_seam(img, seam):
    img_seam_overlay = np.copy(img) x

    # Extract the list of points from the seam
    x_coords, y_coords = np.transpose([(i,int(j)) for i,j in
enumerate(seam)])

    # Draw a green line on the image using the list of points
    img_seam_overlay[x_coords, y_coords] = (0,255,0)
```

```
        return img_seam_overlay

# Compute the energy matrix from the input image
def compute_energy_matrix(img):
    gray = cv2.cvtColor(img, cv2.COLOR_BGR2GRAY)

    # Compute X derivative of the image
    sobel_x = cv2.Sobel(gray,cv2.CV_64F,1,0,ksize=3)

    # Compute Y derivative of the image
    sobel_y = cv2.Sobel(gray,cv2.CV_64F,0,1,ksize=3)

    abs_sobel_x = cv2.convertScaleAbs(sobel_x)
    abs_sobel_y = cv2.convertScaleAbs(sobel_y)

    # Return weighted summation of the two images i.e. 0.5*X +
0.5*Y
    return cv2.addWeighted(abs_sobel_x, 0.5, abs_sobel_y, 0.5, 0)

# Find vertical seam in the input image
def find_vertical_seam(img, energy):
    rows, cols = img.shape[:2]

    # Initialize the seam vector with 0 for each element
    seam = np.zeros(img.shape[0])

    # Initialize distance and edge matrices
    dist_to = np.zeros(img.shape[:2]) + sys.maxint
    dist_to[0,:] = np.zeros(img.shape[1])
    edge_to = np.zeros(img.shape[:2])

    # Dynamic programming; iterate using double loop and compute
the paths efficiently
    for row in xrange(rows-1):
        for col in xrange(cols):
            if col != 0:
                if dist_to[row+1, col-1] > dist_to[row, col] +
energy[row+1, col-1]:
                    dist_to[row+1, col-1] = dist_to[row, col] +
energy[row+1, col-1]
                    edge_to[row+1, col-1] = 1

            if dist_to[row+1, col] > dist_to[row, col] +
energy[row+1, col]:
```

```
                    dist_to[row+1, col] = dist_to[row, col] +
energy[row+1, col]
                    edge_to[row+1, col] = 0

            if col != cols-1:
                if dist_to[row+1, col+1] > dist_to[row, col] +
energy[row+1, col+1]:
                    dist_to[row+1, col+1] = dist_to[row, col] +
energy[row+1, col+1]
                    edge_to[row+1, col+1] = -1

    # Retracing the path
    seam[rows-1] = np.argmin(dist_to[rows-1, :])
    for i in (x for x in reversed(xrange(rows)) if x > 0):
        seam[i-1] = seam[i] + edge_to[i, int(seam[i])]

    return seam

# Remove the input vertical seam from the image
def remove_vertical_seam(img, seam):
    rows, cols = img.shape[:2]

    # To delete a point, move every point after it one step
towards the left
    for row in xrange(rows):
        for col in xrange(int(seam[row]), cols-1):
            img[row, col] = img[row, col+1]

    # Discard the last column to create the final output image
    img = img[:, 0:cols-1]
    return img

if __name__=='__main__':
    # Make sure the size of the input image is reasonable.
    # Large images take a lot of time to be processed.
    # Recommended size is 640x480.
    img_input = cv2.imread(sys.argv[1])

    # Use a small number to get started. Once you get an
    # idea of the processing time, you can use a bigger number.
    # To get started, you can set it to 20.
    num_seams = int(sys.argv[2])
```

```
img = np.copy(img_input)
img_overlay_seam = np.copy(img_input)
energy = compute_energy_matrix(img)

for i in xrange(num_seams):
    seam = find_vertical_seam(img, energy)
    img_overlay_seam = overlay_vertical_seam(img_overlay_seam,
seam)
    img = remove_vertical_seam(img, seam)
    energy = compute_energy_matrix(img)
    print 'Number of seams removed =', i+1

cv2.imshow('Input', img_input)
cv2.imshow('Seams', img_overlay_seam)
cv2.imshow('Output', img)
cv2.waitKey()
```

# Can we expand an image?

We know that we can use seam carving to reduce the width of an image without deteriorating the interesting regions. So naturally, we need to ask ourselves if we can expand an image without deteriorating the interesting regions? As it turns out, we can do it using the same logic. When we compute the seams, we just need to add an extra column instead of deleting it.

If you expand the ducks image naively, it will look something like this:

If you do it in a smarter way, that is, by using seam carving, it will look something like this:

As you can see here, the width of the image has increased and the ducks don't look stretched. Following is the code to do it:

```python
import sys

import cv2
import numpy as np

# Compute the energy matrix from the input image
def compute_energy_matrix(img):
    gray = cv2.cvtColor(img, cv2.COLOR_BGR2GRAY)
    sobel_x = cv2.Sobel(gray, cv2.CV_64F, 1, 0, ksize=3)
    sobel_y = cv2.Sobel(gray, cv2.CV_64F, 0, 1, ksize=3)
    abs_sobel_x = cv2.convertScaleAbs(sobel_x)
    abs_sobel_y = cv2.convertScaleAbs(sobel_y)
    return cv2.addWeighted(abs_sobel_x, 0.5, abs_sobel_y, 0.5, 0)

# Find the vertical seam
def find_vertical_seam(img, energy):
    rows, cols = img.shape[:2]

    # Initialize the seam vector with 0 for each element
    seam = np.zeros(img.shape[0])
```

```
    # Initialize distance and edge matrices
    dist_to = np.zeros(img.shape[:2]) + sys.maxint
    dist_to[0,:] = np.zeros(img.shape[1])
    edge_to = np.zeros(img.shape[:2])

    # Dynamic programming; iterate using double loop and compute
    #the paths efficiently
    for row in xrange(rows-1):
        for col in xrange(cols):
            if col != 0:
                if dist_to[row+1, col-1] > dist_to[row, col] +
                energy[row+1, col-1]:
                    dist_to[row+1, col-1] = dist_to[row, col] +
                    energy[row+1, col-1]
                    edge_to[row+1, col-1] = 1

            if dist_to[row+1, col] > dist_to[row, col] +
            energy[row+1, col]:
                dist_to[row+1, col] = dist_to[row, col] +
                energy[row+1, col]
                edge_to[row+1, col] = 0

            if col != cols-1:
                if dist_to[row+1, col+1] > dist_to[row, col] +
                energy[row+1, col+1]:
                    dist_to[row+1, col+1] = dist_to[row, col] +
                    energy[row+1, col+1]
                    edge_to[row+1, col+1] = -1

    # Retracing the path
    seam[rows-1] = np.argmin(dist_to[rows-1, :])
    for i in (x for x in reversed(xrange(rows)) if x > 0):
        seam[i-1] = seam[i] + edge_to[i, int(seam[i])]

    return seam

# Add a vertical seam to the image
def add_vertical_seam(img, seam, num_iter):
    seam = seam + num_iter
    rows, cols = img.shape[:2]
    zero_col_mat = np.zeros((rows,1,3), dtype=np.uint8)
    img_extended = np.hstack((img, zero_col_mat))
```

```
            for row in xrange(rows):
                for col in xrange(cols, int(seam[row]), -1):
                    img_extended[row, col] = img[row, col-1]

                # To insert a value between two columns, take the average
                # value of the neighbors. It looks smooth this way and we
                # can avoid unwanted artifacts.
                for i in range(3):
                    v1 = img_extended[row, int(seam[row])-1, i]
                    v2 = img_extended[row, int(seam[row])+1, i]
                    img_extended[row, int(seam[row]), i] =
                    (int(v1)+int(v2))/2

        return img_extended

    # Remove vertical seam from the image
    def remove_vertical_seam(img, seam):
        rows, cols = img.shape[:2]
        for row in xrange(rows):
            for col in xrange(int(seam[row]), cols-1):
                img[row, col] = img[row, col+1]

        img = img[:, 0:cols-1]
        return img

    if __name__=='__main__':
        img_input = cv2.imread(sys.argv[1])
        num_seams = int(sys.argv[2])
        img = np.copy(img_input)
        img_output = np.copy(img_input)
        energy = compute_energy_matrix(img)

        for i in xrange(num_seams):
            seam = find_vertical_seam(img, energy)
            img = remove_vertical_seam(img, seam)
            img_output = add_vertical_seam(img_output, seam, i)
            energy = compute_energy_matrix(img)
            print 'Number of seams added =', i+1

        cv2.imshow('Input', img_input)
        cv2.imshow('Output', img_output)
        cv2.waitKey()
```

We added an extra function, `add_vertical_seam`, in this code. We use it to add vertical seams so that the image looks natural.

# Can we remove an object completely?

This is perhaps the most interesting application of seam carving. We can make an object completely disappear from an image. Let's consider the following image:

Let's select the region of interest:

After you remove the chair on the right, it will look something like this:

It's as if the chair never existed! Before we look at the code, it's important to know that this takes a while to run. So, just wait for a couple of minutes to get an idea of the processing time. You can adjust the input image size accordingly! Let's take a look at the code:

```python
import sys

import cv2
import numpy as np

# Draw rectangle on top of the input image
def draw_rectangle(event, x, y, flags, params):
    global x_init, y_init, drawing, top_left_pt, bottom_right_pt,
    img_orig

    # Detecting a mouse click
    if event == cv2.EVENT_LBUTTONDOWN:
        drawing = True
        x_init, y_init = x, y

    # Detecting mouse movement
    elif event == cv2.EVENT_MOUSEMOVE:
        if drawing:
            top_left_pt, bottom_right_pt = (x_init,y_init), (x,y)
            img[y_init:y, x_init:x] = 255 - img_orig[y_init:y,
            x_init:x]
```

```
        cv2.rectangle(img, top_left_pt, bottom_right_pt,
        (0,255,0), 2)

    # Detecting the mouse button up event
    elif event == cv2.EVENT_LBUTTONUP:
        drawing = False
        top_left_pt, bottom_right_pt = (x_init,y_init), (x,y)

        # Create the "negative" film effect for the selected
        # region
        img[y_init:y, x_init:x] = 255 - img[y_init:y, x_init:x]

        # Draw rectangle around the selected region
        cv2.rectangle(img, top_left_pt, bottom_right_pt,
        (0,255,0), 2)
        rect_final = (x_init, y_init, x-x_init, y-y_init)

        # Remove the object in the selected region
        remove_object(img_orig, rect_final)

# Computing the energy matrix using modified algorithm
def compute_energy_matrix_modified(img, rect_roi):
    gray = cv2.cvtColor(img, cv2.COLOR_BGR2GRAY)

    # Compute the X derivative
    sobel_x = cv2.Sobel(gray,cv2.CV_64F,1,0,ksize=3)

    # Compute the Y derivative
    sobel_y = cv2.Sobel(gray,cv2.CV_64F,0,1,ksize=3)
    abs_sobel_x = cv2.convertScaleAbs(sobel_x)
    abs_sobel_y = cv2.convertScaleAbs(sobel_y)

    # Compute weighted summation i.e. 0.5*X + 0.5*Y
    energy_matrix = cv2.addWeighted(abs_sobel_x, 0.5, abs_sobel_y,
    0.5, 0)
    x,y,w,h = rect_roi

    # We want the seams to pass through this region, so make sure the
energy values in this region are set to 0
    energy_matrix[y:y+h, x:x+w] = 0

    return energy_matrix
```

```python
# Compute energy matrix
def compute_energy_matrix(img):
    gray = cv2.cvtColor(img, cv2.COLOR_BGR2GRAY)

    # Compute X derivative
    sobel_x = cv2.Sobel(gray, cv2.CV_64F, 1, 0, ksize=3)

    # Compute Y derivative
    sobel_y = cv2.Sobel(gray, cv2.CV_64F, 0, 1, ksize=3)
    abs_sobel_x = cv2.convertScaleAbs(sobel_x)
    abs_sobel_y = cv2.convertScaleAbs(sobel_y)

    # Return weighted summation i.e. 0.5*X + 0.5*Y
    return cv2.addWeighted(abs_sobel_x, 0.5, abs_sobel_y, 0.5, 0)

# Find the vertical seam
def find_vertical_seam(img, energy):
    rows, cols = img.shape[:2]

    # Initialize the seam vector
    seam = np.zeros(img.shape[0])

    # Initialize the distance and edge matrices
    dist_to = np.zeros(img.shape[:2]) + sys.maxint
    dist_to[0,:] = np.zeros(img.shape[1])
    edge_to = np.zeros(img.shape[:2])

    # Dynamic programming; using double loop to compute the paths
    for row in xrange(rows-1):
        for col in xrange(cols):
            if col != 0:
                if dist_to[row+1, col-1] > dist_to[row, col] +
                energy[row+1, col-1]:
                    dist_to[row+1, col-1] = dist_to[row, col] +
                    energy[row+1, col-1]
                    edge_to[row+1, col-1] = 1

            if dist_to[row+1, col] > dist_to[row, col] +
            energy[row+1, col]:
                dist_to[row+1, col] = dist_to[row, col] +
                energy[row+1, col]
                edge_to[row+1, col] = 0
```

```
                 if col != cols-1:
                     if dist_to[row+1, col+1] > dist_to[row, col] +
                     energy[row+1, col+1]:
                         dist_to[row+1, col+1] = dist_to[row, col] +
                         energy[row+1, col+1]
                         edge_to[row+1, col+1] = -1

    # Retracing the path
    seam[rows-1] = np.argmin(dist_to[rows-1, :])
    for i in (x for x in reversed(xrange(rows)) if x > 0):
        seam[i-1] = seam[i] + edge_to[i, int(seam[i])]

    return seam

# Add vertical seam to the input image
def add_vertical_seam(img, seam, num_iter):
    seam = seam + num_iter
    rows, cols = img.shape[:2]
    zero_col_mat = np.zeros((rows,1,3), dtype=np.uint8)
    img_extended = np.hstack((img, zero_col_mat))

    for row in xrange(rows):
        for col in xrange(cols, int(seam[row]), -1):
            img_extended[row, col] = img[row, col-1]

        # To insert a value between two columns, take the average
        # value of the neighbors. It looks smooth this way and we
        # can avoid unwanted artifacts.
        for i in range(3):
            v1 = img_extended[row, int(seam[row])-1, i]
            v2 = img_extended[row, int(seam[row])+1, i]
            img_extended[row, int(seam[row]), i] = (int(v1)+int(v2))/2

    return img_extended

# Remove vertical seam
def remove_vertical_seam(img, seam):
    rows, cols = img.shape[:2]
    for row in xrange(rows):
        for col in xrange(int(seam[row]), cols-1):
            img[row, col] = img[row, col+1]

    img = img[:, 0:cols-1]
    return img
```

```python
# Remove the object from the input region of interest
def remove_object(img, rect_roi):
    num_seams = rect_roi[2] + 10
    energy = compute_energy_matrix_modified(img, rect_roi)

    # Start a loop and remove one seam at a time
    for i in xrange(num_seams):
        # Find the vertical seam that can be removed
        seam = find_vertical_seam(img, energy)

        # Remove that vertical seam
        img = remove_vertical_seam(img, seam)
        x,y,w,h = rect_roi

        # Compute energy matrix after removing the seam
        energy = compute_energy_matrix_modified(img, (x,y,w-i,h))
        print 'Number of seams removed =', i+1

    img_output = np.copy(img)

    # Fill up the region with surrounding values so that the size
    # of the image remains unchanged
    for i in xrange(num_seams):
        seam = find_vertical_seam(img, energy)
        img = remove_vertical_seam(img, seam)
        img_output = add_vertical_seam(img_output, seam, i)
        energy = compute_energy_matrix(img)
        print 'Number of seams added =', i+1

    cv2.imshow('Input', img_input)
    cv2.imshow('Output', img_output)
    cv2.waitKey()

if __name__=='__main__':
    img_input = cv2.imread(sys.argv[1])

    drawing = False
    img = np.copy(img_input)
    img_orig = np.copy(img_input)

    cv2.namedWindow('Input')
    cv2.setMouseCallback('Input', draw_rectangle)
```

```
while True:
    cv2.imshow('Input', img)
    c = cv2.waitKey(10)
    if c == 27:
        break

cv2.destroyAllWindows()
```

# How did we do it?

The basic logic remains the same here. We are using seam carving to remove an object. Once we select the region of interest, we make all the seams pass through this region. We do this by manipulating the energy matrix after every iteration. We have added a new function called `compute_energy_matrix_modified` to achieve this. Once we compute the energy matrix, we assign a value of 0 to this region of interest. This way, we force all the seams to pass through this area. After we remove all the seams related to this region, we keep adding the seams until we expand the image to its original width.

# Summary

In this chapter, we learned about content-aware image resizing. We discussed how to quantify interesting and uninteresting regions in an image. We learned how to compute seams in an image and how to use dynamic programming to do it efficiently. We discussed how to use seam carving to reduce the width of an image, and how we can use the same logic to expand an image. We also learned how to remove an object from an image completely.

In the next chapter, we are going to discuss how to do shape analysis and image segmentation. We will see how to use those principles to find the exact boundaries of an object of interest in the image.

# 8

# Detecting Shapes and Segmenting an Image

In this chapter, we are going to learn about shape analysis and image segmentation. We will learn how to recognize shapes and estimate the exact boundaries. We will discuss how to segment an image into its constituent parts using various methods. We will learn how to separate the foreground from the background as well.

By the end of this chapter, you will know:

- What is contour analysis and shape matching
- How to match shapes
- What is image segmentation
- How to segment an image into its constituent parts
- How to separate the foreground from the background
- How to use various techniques to segment an image

## Contour analysis and shape matching

Contour analysis is a very useful tool in the field of computer vision. We deal with a lot of shapes in the real world and contour analysis helps in analyzing those shapes using various algorithms. When we convert an image to grayscale and threshold it, we are left with a bunch of lines and contours. Once we understand the properties of different shapes, we will be able to extract detailed information from an image.

Let's say we want to identify the boomerang shape in the following image:

In order to do that, we first need to know what a regular boomerang looks like:

Now using the above image as a reference, can we identify what shape in our original image corresponds to a boomerang? If you notice, we cannot use a simple correlation based approach because the shapes are all distorted. This means that an approach where we look for an exact match won't work! We need to understand the properties of this shape and match the corresponding properties to identify the boomerang shape. OpenCV provides a nice shape matcher function that we can use to achieve this. The matching is based on the concept of Hu moment, which in turn is related to image moments. You can refer to the following paper to learn more about moments: `http://zoi.utia.cas.cz/files/chapter_moments_color1.pdf`. The concept of "image moments" basically refers to the weighted and power-raised summation of the pixels within a shape.

$$I = \sum_{i=0}^{N} w_i p_i^k$$

In the above equation, **p** refers to the pixels inside the contour, **w** refers to the weights, **N** refers to the number of points inside the contour, **k** refers to the power, and **I** refers to the moment. Depending on the values we choose for w and k, we can extract different characteristics from that contour.

Perhaps the simplest example is to compute the area of the contour. To do this, we need to count the number of pixels within that region. So mathematically speaking, in the weighted and power raised summation form, we just need to set w to 1 and k to 0. This will give us the area of the contour. Depending on how we compute these moments, they will help us in understanding these different shapes. This also gives rise to some interesting properties that help us in determining the shape similarity metric.

If we match the shapes, you will see something like this:

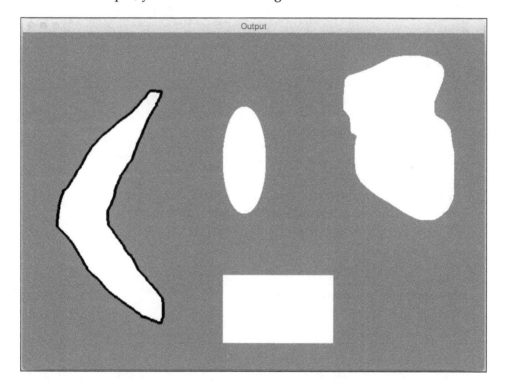

Let's take a look at the code to do this:

```
import sys

import cv2
import numpy as np
```

```
# Extract reference contour from the image
def get_ref_contour(img):
    ref_gray = cv2.cvtColor(img, cv2.COLOR_BGR2GRAY)
    ret, thresh = cv2.threshold(ref_gray, 127, 255, 0)

    # Find all the contours in the thresholded image. The values
    # for the second and third parameters are restricted to a
    # certain number of possible values. You can learn more
    # 'findContours' function here: http://docs.opencv.org/modules/
imgproc/doc/structural_analysis_and_shape_descriptors.html
    contours, hierarchy = cv2.findContours(thresh, 1, 2)

    # Extract the relevant contour based on area ratio. We use the
    # area ratio because the main image boundary contour is
    # extracted as well and we don't want that. This area ratio
    # threshold will ensure that we only take the contour inside
    # the image.
    for contour in contours:
        area = cv2.contourArea(contour)
        img_area = img.shape[0] * img.shape[1]
        if 0.05 < area/float(img_area) < 0.8:
            return contour

# Extract all the contours from the image
def get_all_contours(img):
    ref_gray = cv2.cvtColor(img, cv2.COLOR_BGR2GRAY)
    ret, thresh = cv2.threshold(ref_gray, 127, 255, 0)
    contours, hierarchy = cv2.findContours(thresh, 1, 2)
    return contours

if __name__=='__main__':
    # Boomerang reference image
    img1 = cv2.imread(sys.argv[1])

    # Input image containing all the different shapes
    img2 = cv2.imread(sys.argv[2])

    # Extract the reference contour
    ref_contour = get_ref_contour(img1)

    # Extract all the contours from the input image
    input_contours = get_all_contours(img2)

    closest_contour = input_contours[0]
    min_dist = sys.maxint
```

```
# Finding the closest contour
for contour in input_contours:
    # Matching the shapes and taking the closest one
    ret = cv2.matchShapes(ref_contour, contour, 1, 0.0)
    if ret < min_dist:
        min_dist = ret
        closest_contour = contour

cv2.drawContours(img2, [closest_contour], -1, (0,0,0), 3)
cv2.imshow('Output', img2)
cv2.waitKey()
```

# Approximating a contour

A lot of contours that we encounter in real life are noisy. This means that the contours don't look smooth, and hence our analysis takes a hit. So how do we deal with this? One way to go about this would be to get all the points on the contour and then approximate it with a smooth polygon.

Let's consider the boomerang image again. If you approximate the contours using various thresholds, you will see the contours changing their shapes. Let's start with a factor of 0.05:

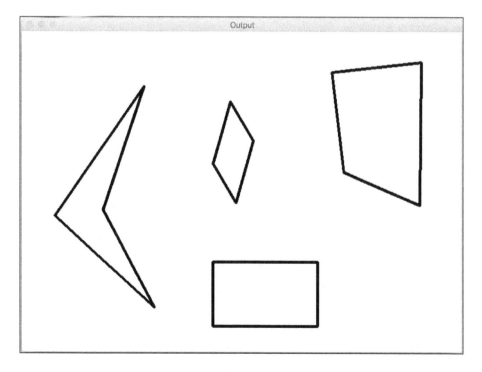

If you reduce this factor, the contours will get smoother. Let's make it 0.01:

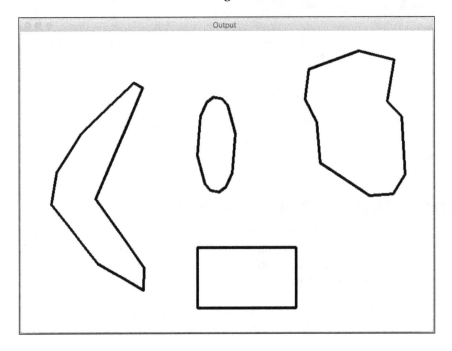

If you make it really small, say 0.00001, then it will look like the original image:

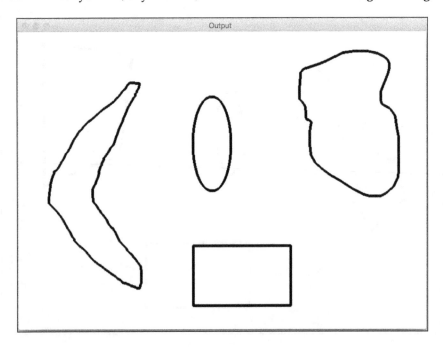

# Identifying the pizza with the slice taken out

The title might be slightly misleading, because we will not be talking about pizza slices. But let's say you are in a situation where you have an image containing different types of pizzas with different shapes. Now, somebody has taken a slice out of one of those pizzas. How would we automatically identify this?

We cannot take the approach we took earlier because we don't know what the shape looks like. So we don't have any template. We are not even sure what shape we are looking for, so we cannot build a template based on any prior information. All we know is the fact that a slice has been taken from one of the pizzas. Let's consider the following image:

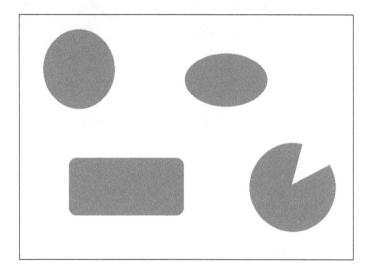

It's not exactly a real image, but you get the idea. You know what shape we are talking about. Since we don't know what we are looking for, we need to use some of the properties of these shapes to identify the sliced pizza. If you notice, all the other shapes are nicely closed. As in, you can take any two points within those shapes and draw a line between them, and that line will always lie within that shape. These kinds of shapes are called **convex shapes**.

If you look at the sliced pizza shape, we can choose two points such that the line between them goes outside the shape as shown in the figure that follows:

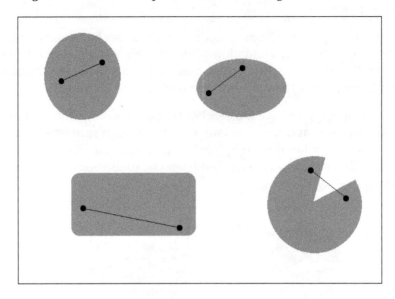

So, all we need to do is detect the non-convex shape in the image and we'll be done. Let's go ahead and do that:

```python
import sys

import cv2
import numpy as np

# Input is a color image
def get_contours(img):
    # Convert the image to grayscale
    img_gray = cv2.cvtColor(img, cv2.COLOR_BGR2GRAY)

    # Threshold the input image
    ret, thresh = cv2.threshold(img_gray, 127, 255, 0)

    # Find the contours in the above image
    contours, hierarchy = cv2.findContours(thresh, 2, 1)

    return contours

if __name__=='__main__':
    img = cv2.imread(sys.argv[1])
```

```
# Iterate over the extracted contours
for contour in get_contours(img):
    # Extract convex hull from the contour
    hull = cv2.convexHull(contour, returnPoints=False)

    # Extract convexity defects from the above hull
    defects = cv2.convexityDefects(contour, hull)

    if defects is None:
        continue

    # Draw lines and circles to show the defects
    for i in range(defects.shape[0]):
        start_defect, end_defect, far_defect, _ = defects[i,0]
        start = tuple(contour[start_defect][0])
        end = tuple(contour[end_defect][0])
        far = tuple(contour[far_defect][0])
        cv2.circle(img, far, 5, [128,0,0], -1)
        cv2.drawContours(img, [contour], -1, (0,0,0), 3)

cv2.imshow('Convexity defects',img)
cv2.waitKey(0)
cv2.destroyAllWindows()
```

If you run the above code, you will see something like this:

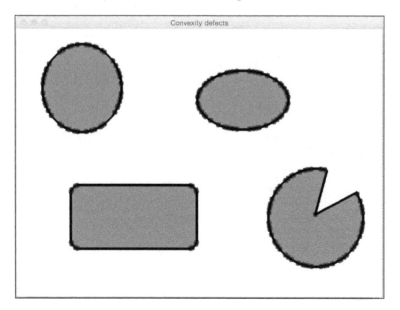

Wait a minute, what happened here? It looks so cluttered. Did we do something wrong? As it turns out, the curves are not really smooth. If you observe closely, there are tiny ridges everywhere along the curves. So, if you just run your convexity detector, it's not going to work. This is where contour approximation comes in really handy. Once we've detected the contours, we need to smoothen them so that the ridges do not affect them. Let's go ahead and do that:

```python
import sys

import cv2
import numpy as np

# Input is a color image
def get_contours(img):
    img_gray = cv2.cvtColor(img, cv2.COLOR_BGR2GRAY)
    ret, thresh = cv2.threshold(img_gray, 127, 255, 0)
    contours, hierarchy = cv2.findContours(thresh, 2, 1)
    return contours

if __name__=='__main__':
    img = cv2.imread(sys.argv[1])

    # Iterate over the extracted contours
    for contour in get_contours(img):
        orig_contour = contour
        epsilon = 0.01 * cv2.arcLength(contour, True)
        contour = cv2.approxPolyDP(contour, epsilon, True)

        # Extract convex hull and the convexity defects
        hull = cv2.convexHull(contour, returnPoints=False)
        defects = cv2.convexityDefects(contour,hull)

        if defects is None:
            continue

        # Draw lines and circles to show the defects
        for i in range(defects.shape[0]):
            start_defect, end_defect, far_defect, _ = defects[i,0]
            start = tuple(contour[start_defect][0])
            end = tuple(contour[end_defect][0])
            far = tuple(contour[far_defect][0])
            cv2.circle(img, far, 7, [255,0,0], -1)
            cv2.drawContours(img, [orig_contour], -1, (0,0,0), 3)

    cv2.imshow('Convexity defects',img)
    cv2.waitKey(0)
    cv2.destroyAllWindows()
```

If you run the preceding code, the output will look like the following:

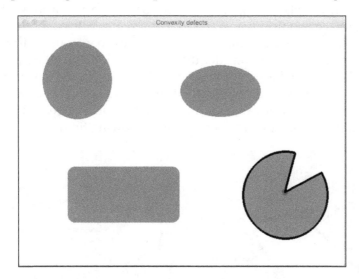

# How to censor a shape?

Let's say you are dealing with images and you want to block out a particular shape. Now, you might say that you will use shape matching to identify the shape and then just block it out, right? But the problem here is that we don't have any template available. So, how do we go about doing this? Shape analysis comes in various forms, and we need to build our algorithm depending on the situation. Let's consider the following figure:

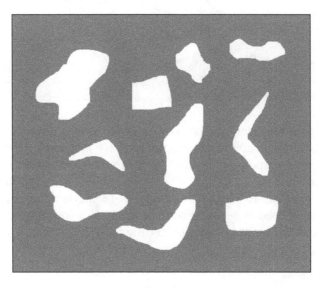

Let's say we want to identify all the boomerang shapes and then block them out without using any template images. As you can see, there are various other weird shapes in that image and the boomerang shapes are not really smooth. We need to identify the property that's going to differentiate the boomerang shape from the other shapes present. Let's consider the convex hull. If you take the ratio of the area of each shape to the area of the convex hull, we can see that this can be a distinguishing metric. This metric is called **solidity factor** in shape analysis. This metric will have a lower value for the boomerang shapes because of the empty area that will be left out, as shown in the following figure:

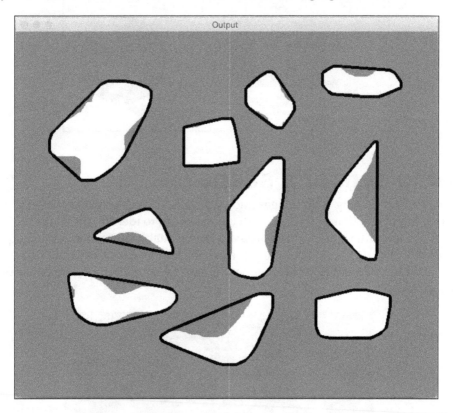

The black boundaries represent the convex hulls. Once we compute these values for all the shapes, how do separate them out? Can we just use a fixed threshold to detect the boomerang shapes? Not really! We cannot have a fixed threshold value because you never know what kind of shape you might encounter later. So, a better approach would be to use **K-Means clustering**. K-Means is an unsupervised learning technique that can be used to separate out the input data into K classes. You can quickly brush up on K-Means before proceeding further at http://docs.opencv.org/master/de/d4d/tutorial_py_kmeans_understanding.html.

We know that we want to separate the shapes into two groups, that is, boomerang shapes and other shapes. So, we know what our *K* will be in K-Means. Once we use that and cluster the values, we pick the cluster with the lowest solidity factor and that will give us our boomerang shapes. Bear in mind that this approach works only in this particular case. If you are dealing with other kinds of shapes, then you will have to use some other metrics to make sure that the shape detection works. As we discussed earlier, it depends heavily on the situation. If you detect the shapes and block them out, it will look like this:

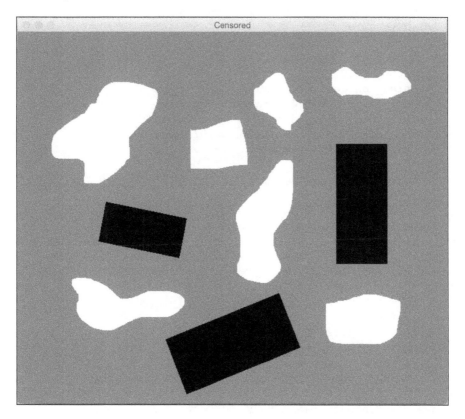

Following is the code to do it:

```
import sys

import cv2
import numpy as np

def get_all_contours(img):
    ref_gray = cv2.cvtColor(img, cv2.COLOR_BGR2GRAY)
```

```python
    ret, thresh = cv2.threshold(ref_gray, 127, 255, 0)
    contours, hierarchy = cv2.findContours(thresh, 1, 2)
    return contours

if __name__=='__main__':
    # Input image containing all the shapes
    img = cv2.imread(sys.argv[1])

    img_orig = np.copy(img)
    input_contours = get_all_contours(img)
    solidity_values = []

    # Compute solidity factors of all the contours
    for contour in input_contours:
        area_contour = cv2.contourArea(contour)
        convex_hull = cv2.convexHull(contour)
        area_hull = cv2.contourArea(convex_hull)
        solidity = float(area_contour)/area_hull
        solidity_values.append(solidity)

    # Clustering using KMeans
    criteria = (cv2.TERM_CRITERIA_EPS +
cv2.TERM_CRITERIA_MAX_ITER, 10, 1.0)
    flags = cv2.KMEANS_RANDOM_CENTERS
    solidity_values = np.array(solidity_values).reshape((len(solidity_
values),1)).astype('float32')
    compactness, labels, centers = cv2.kmeans(solidity_values, 2,
criteria, 10, flags)

    closest_class = np.argmin(centers)
    output_contours = []
    for i in solidity_values[labels==closest_class]:
        index = np.where(solidity_values==i)[0][0]
        output_contours.append(input_contours[index])

    cv2.drawContours(img, output_contours, -1, (0,0,0), 3)
    cv2.imshow('Output', img)

    # Censoring
    for contour in output_contours:
        rect = cv2.minAreaRect(contour)
        box = cv2.cv.BoxPoints(rect)
        box = np.int0(box)
        cv2.drawContours(img_orig, [box],0,(0,0,0),-1)

    cv2.imshow('Censored', img_orig)
    cv2.waitKey()
```

# What is image segmentation?

Image segmentation is the process of separating an image into its constituent parts. It is an important step in many computer vision applications in the real world. There are many different ways of segmenting an image. When we segment an image, we separate the regions based on various metrics such as color, texture, location, and so on. All the pixels within each region have something in common, depending on the metric we are using. Let's take a look at some of the popular approaches here.

To start with, we will be looking at a technique called **GrabCut**. It is an image segmentation method based on a more generic approach called **graph-cuts**. In the graph-cuts method, we consider the entire image to be a graph, and then we segment the graph based on the strength of the edges in that graph. We construct the graph by considering each pixel to be a node and edges are constructed between the nodes, where edge weight is a function of the pixel values of those two nodes. Whenever there is a boundary, the pixel values are higher. Hence, the edge weights will also be higher. This graph is then segmented by minimizing the Gibss energy of the graph. This is analogous to finding the maximum entropy segmentation. You can refer to the original paper to learn more about it at `http://cvg.ethz.ch/teaching/cvl/2012/grabcut-siggraph04.pdf`. Let's consider the following image:

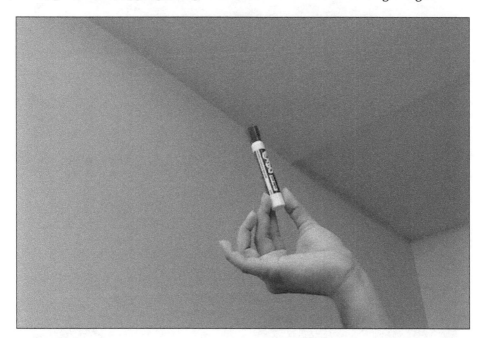

Let's select the region of interest:

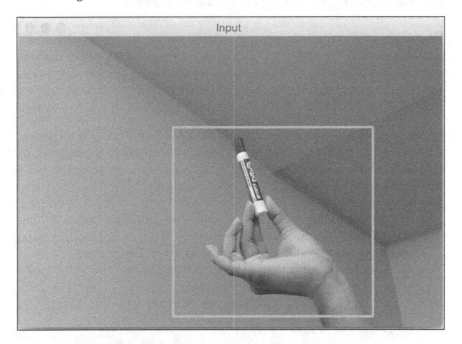

Once the image has been segmented, it will look something like this:

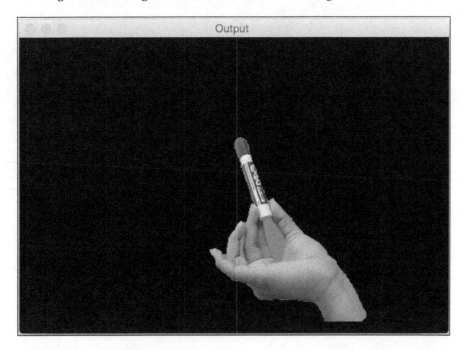

Following is the code to do this:

```
import cv2
import numpy as np

# Draw rectangle based on the input selection
def draw_rectangle(event, x, y, flags, params):
    global x_init, y_init, drawing, top_left_pt, bottom_right_pt,
    img_orig

    # Detecting mouse button down event
    if event == cv2.EVENT_LBUTTONDOWN:
        drawing = True
        x_init, y_init = x, y

    # Detecting mouse movement
    elif event == cv2.EVENT_MOUSEMOVE:
        if drawing:
            top_left_pt, bottom_right_pt = (x_init,y_init), (x,y)
            img[y_init:y, x_init:x] = 255 - img_orig[y_init:y,
            x_init:x]
            cv2.rectangle(img, top_left_pt, bottom_right_pt,
            (0,255,0), 2)

    # Detecting mouse button up event
    elif event == cv2.EVENT_LBUTTONUP:
        drawing = False
        top_left_pt, bottom_right_pt = (x_init,y_init), (x,y)
        img[y_init:y, x_init:x] = 255 - img[y_init:y, x_init:x]
        cv2.rectangle(img, top_left_pt, bottom_right_pt,
        (0,255,0), 2)
        rect_final = (x_init, y_init, x-x_init, y-y_init)

        # Run Grabcut on the region of interest
        run_grabcut(img_orig, rect_final)

# Grabcut algorithm
def run_grabcut(img_orig, rect_final):
    # Initialize the mask
    mask = np.zeros(img_orig.shape[:2],np.uint8)

    # Extract the rectangle and set the region of
    # interest in the above mask
    x,y,w,h = rect_final
```

```
        mask[y:y+h, x:x+w] = 1

        # Initialize background and foreground models
        bgdModel = np.zeros((1,65), np.float64)
        fgdModel = np.zeros((1,65), np.float64)

        # Run Grabcut algorithm
        cv2.grabCut(img_orig, mask, rect_final, bgdModel, fgdModel, 5,
        cv2.GC_INIT_WITH_RECT)

        # Extract new mask
        mask2 = np.where((mask==2)|(mask==0),0,1).astype('uint8')

        # Apply the above mask to the image
        img_orig = img_orig*mask2[:,:,np.newaxis]

        # Display the image
        cv2.imshow('Output', img_orig)

if __name__=='__main__':
    drawing = False
    top_left_pt, bottom_right_pt = (-1,-1), (-1,-1)

    # Read the input image
    img_orig = cv2.imread(sys.argv[1])
    img = img_orig.copy()

    cv2.namedWindow('Input')
    cv2.setMouseCallback('Input', draw_rectangle)

    while True:
        cv2.imshow('Input', img)
        c = cv2.waitKey(1)
        if c == 27:
            break

    cv2.destroyAllWindows()
```

# How does it work?

We start with the seed points specified by the user. This is the bounding box within which we have the object of interest. Underneath the surface, the algorithm estimates the color distribution of the object and the background. The algorithm represents the color distribution of the image as a **Gaussian Mixture Markov Random Field (GMMRF)**. You can refer to the detailed paper to learn more about GMMRF at `http://research.microsoft.com/pubs/67898/eccv04-GMMRF.pdf`. We need the color distribution of both, the object and the background, because we will be using this knowledge to separate the object. This information is used to find the maximum entropy segmentation by applying the min-cut algorithm to the Markov Random Field. Once we have this, we use the graph cuts optimization method to infer the labels.

# Watershed algorithm

OpenCV comes with a default implementation of the watershed algorithm. It's pretty famous and there are a lot of implementations available out there. You can read more about it at `http://docs.opencv.org/master/d3/db4/tutorial_py_watershed.html`. Since you already have access to the OpenCV source code, we will not be looking at the code here.

We will just see what the output looks like. Consider the following image:

Let's select the regions:

If you run the watershed algorithm on this, the output will look something like the following:

# Summary

In this chapter, we learned about contour analysis and image segmentation. We learned how to match shapes based on a template. We learned about the various different properties of shapes and how we can use them to identify different kinds of shapes. We discussed image segmentation and how we can use graph-based methods to segment regions in an image. We briefly discussed watershed transformation as well.

In the next chapter, we are going to discuss how to track an object in a live video.

# Object Tracking
# 9

In this chapter, we are going to learn about tracking an object in a live video. We will discuss the different characteristics that can be used to track an object. We will also learn about the different methods and techniques for object tracking.

By the end of this chapter, you will know:

- How to use frame differencing
- How to use colorspaces to track colored objects
- How to build an interactive object tracker
- How to build a feature tracker
- How to build a video surveillance system

## Frame differencing

This is, possibly, the simplest technique we can use to see what parts of the video are moving. When we consider a live video stream, the difference between successive frames gives us a lot of information. The concept is fairly straightforward! We just take the difference between successive frames and display the differences.

If I move my laptop rapidly from left to right, we will see something like this:

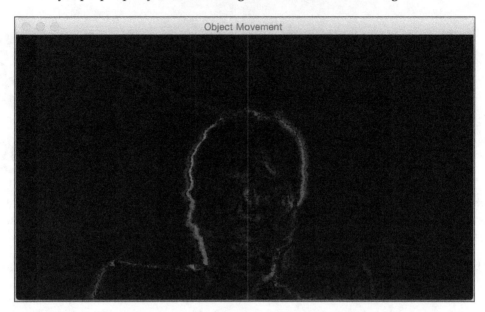

If I rapidly move the TV remote in my hand, it will look something like this:

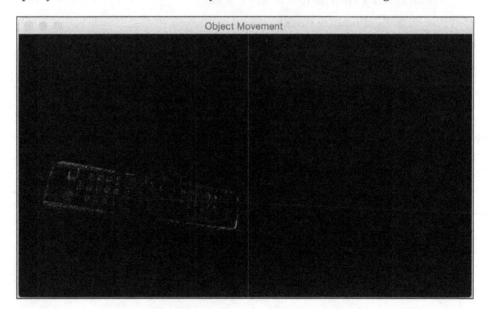

As you can see from the previous images, only the moving parts in the video get highlighted. This gives us a good starting point to see what areas are moving in the video. Here is the code to do this:

```python
import cv2

# Compute the frame difference
def frame_diff(prev_frame, cur_frame, next_frame):
    # Absolute difference between current frame and next frame
    diff_frames1 = cv2.absdiff(next_frame, cur_frame)

    # Absolute difference between current frame and
    # previous frame
    diff_frames2 = cv2.absdiff(cur_frame, prev_frame)

    # Return the result of bitwise 'AND' between the
    # above two resultant images
    return cv2.bitwise_and(diff_frames1, diff_frames2)

# Capture the frame from webcam
def get_frame(cap):
    # Capture the frame
    ret, frame = cap.read()

    # Resize the image
    frame = cv2.resize(frame, None, fx=scaling_factor,
            fy=scaling_factor, interpolation=cv2.INTER_AREA)

    # Return the grayscale image
    return cv2.cvtColor(frame, cv2.COLOR_RGB2GRAY)

if __name__=='__main__':
    cap = cv2.VideoCapture(0)
    scaling_factor = 0.5

    prev_frame = get_frame(cap)
    cur_frame = get_frame(cap)
    next_frame = get_frame(cap)

    # Iterate until the user presses the ESC key
    while True:
        # Display the result of frame differencing
        cv2.imshow("Object Movement", frame_diff(prev_frame,
        cur_frame, next_frame))
```

```
        # Update the variables
        prev_frame = cur_frame
        cur_frame = next_frame
        next_frame = get_frame(cap)

        # Check if the user pressed ESC
        key = cv2.waitKey(10)
        if key == 27:
            break

    cv2.destroyAllWindows()
```

# Colorspace based tracking

Frame differencing gives us some useful information, but we cannot use it to build anything meaningful. In order to build a good object tracker, we need to understand what characteristics can be used to make our tracking robust and accurate. So, let's take a step in that direction and see how we can use **colorspaces** to come up with a good tracker. As we have discussed in previous chapters, HSVcolorspace is very informative when it comes to human perception. We can convert an image to the HSV space, and then use colorspacethresholding to track a given object.

Consider the following frame in the video:

If you run it through the colorspace filter and track the object, you will see something like this:

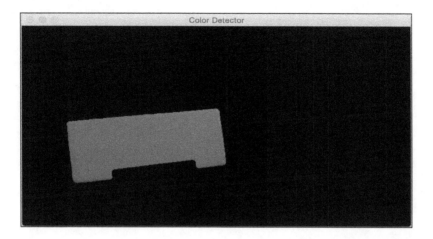

As we can see here, our tracker recognizes a particular object in the video, based on the color characteristics. In order to use this tracker, we need to know the color distribution of our target object. Following is the code:

```
import cv2
import numpy as np

# Capture the input frame from webcam
def get_frame(cap, scaling_factor):
    # Capture the frame from video capture object
    ret, frame = cap.read()

    # Resize the input frame
    frame = cv2.resize(frame, None, fx=scaling_factor,
            fy=scaling_factor, interpolation=cv2.INTER_AREA)

    return frame

if __name__=='__main__':
    cap = cv2.VideoCapture(0)
    scaling_factor = 0.5

    # Iterate until the user presses ESC key
    while True:
        frame = get_frame(cap, scaling_factor)
```

```
# Convert the HSV colorspace
hsv = cv2.cvtColor(frame, cv2.COLOR_BGR2HSV)

# Define 'blue' range in HSV colorspace
lower = np.array([60,100,100])
upper = np.array([180,255,255])

# Threshold the HSV image to get only blue color
mask = cv2.inRange(hsv, lower, upper)

# Bitwise-AND mask and original image
res = cv2.bitwise_and(frame, frame, mask=mask)
res = cv2.medianBlur(res, 5)

cv2.imshow('Original image', frame)
cv2.imshow('Color Detector', res)

# Check if the user pressed ESC key
c = cv2.waitKey(5)
if c == 27:
    break

cv2.destroyAllWindows()
```

# Building an interactive object tracker

Colorspace based tracker gives us the freedom to track a colored object, but we are also constrained to a predefined color. What if we just want to pick an object at random? How do we build an object tracker that can learn the characteristics of the selected object and just track it automatically? This is where the **CAMShift** algorithm, which stands for Continuously Adaptive Meanshift, comes into the picture. It's basically an improved version of the **Meanshift** algorithm.

The concept of Meanshift is actually nice and simple. Let's say we select a region of interest and we want our object tracker to track that object. In that region, we select a bunch of points based on the color histogram and compute the centroid. If the centroid lies at the center of this region, we know that the object hasn't moved. But if the centroid is not at the center of this region, then we know that the object is moving in some direction. The movement of the centroid controls the direction in which the object is moving. So, we move our bounding box to a new location so that the new centroid becomes the center of this bounding box. Hence, this algorithm is called Meanshift, because the mean (i.e. the centroid) is shifting. This way, we keep ourselves updated with the current location of the object.

But the problem with Meanshift is that the size of the bounding box is not allowed to change. When you move the object away from the camera, the object will appear smaller to the human eye, but Meanshift will not take this into account. The size of the bounding box will remain the same throughout the tracking session. Hence, we need to use CAMShift. The advantage of CAMShift is that it can adapt the size of the bounding box to the size of the object. Along with that, it can also keep track of the orientation of the object.

Let's consider the following frame in which the object is highlighted in orange (the box in my hand):

Now that we have selected the object, the algorithm computes the histogram `backprojection` and extracts all the information. Let's move the object and see how it's getting tracked:

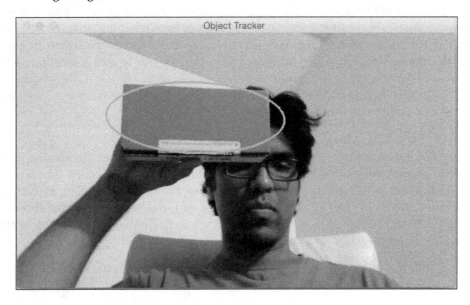

Looks like the object is getting tracked fairly well. Let's change the orientation and see if the tracking is maintained:

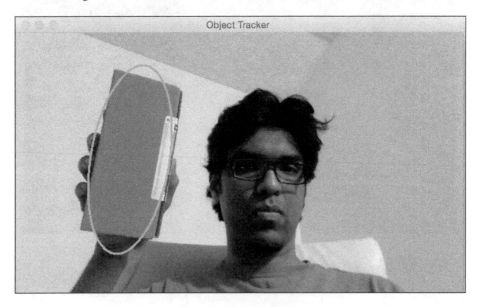

As we can see, the bounding ellipse has changed its location as well as its orientation. Let's change the perspective of the object and see if it's still able to track it:

We are still good! The bounding ellipse has changed the aspect ratio to reflect the fact that the object looks skewed now (because of the perspective transformation).

Following is the code:

```
import sys

import cv2
import numpy as np

class ObjectTracker(object):
    def __init__(self):
        # Initialize the video capture object
        # 0 -> indicates that frame should be captured
        # from webcam
        self.cap = cv2.VideoCapture(0)

        # Capture the frame from the webcam
        ret, self.frame = self.cap.read()

        # Downsampling factor for the input frame
        self.scaling_factor = 0.5
        self.frame = cv2.resize(self.frame, None,
        fx=self.scaling_factor,
```

```python
                    fy=self.scaling_factor,
                    interpolation=cv2.INTER_AREA)

        cv2.namedWindow('Object Tracker')
        cv2.setMouseCallback('Object Tracker',
        self.mouse_event)

        self.selection = None
        self.drag_start = None
        self.tracking_state = 0

    # Method to track mouse events
    def mouse_event(self, event, x, y, flags, param):
        x, y = np.int16([x, y])

        # Detecting the mouse button down event
        if event == cv2.EVENT_LBUTTONDOWN:
            self.drag_start = (x, y)
            self.tracking_state = 0

        if self.drag_start:
            if flags & cv2.EVENT_FLAG_LBUTTON:
                h, w = self.frame.shape[:2]
                xo, yo = self.drag_start
                x0, y0 = np.maximum(0, np.minimum([xo, yo],
                [x, y]))
                x1, y1 = np.minimum([w, h],
                np.maximum([xo, yo], [x, y]))
                self.selection = None

                if x1-x0 > 0 and y1-y0 > 0:
                    self.selection = (x0, y0, x1, y1)

            else:
                self.drag_start = None
                if self.selection is not None:
                    self.tracking_state = 1

    # Method to start tracking the object
    def start_tracking(self):
        # Iterate until the user presses the Esc key
        while True:
            # Capture the frame from webcam
            ret, self.frame = self.cap.read()
```

```python
# Resize the input frame
self.frame = cv2.resize(self.frame, None,
fx=self.scaling_factor,
            fy=self.scaling_factor,
            interpolation=cv2.INTER_AREA)

vis = self.frame.copy()

# Convert to HSV colorspace
hsv = cv2.cvtColor(self.frame, cv2.COLOR_BGR2HSV)

# Create the mask based on predefined thresholds.
mask = cv2.inRange(hsv, np.array((0., 60., 32.)),
            np.array((180., 255., 255.)))

if self.selection:
    x0, y0, x1, y1 = self.selection
    self.track_window = (x0, y0, x1-x0, y1-y0)
    hsv_roi = hsv[y0:y1, x0:x1]
    mask_roi = mask[y0:y1, x0:x1]

    # Compute the histogram
    hist = cv2.calcHist( [hsv_roi], [0], mask_roi,
    [16], [0, 180] )

    # Normalize and reshape the histogram
    cv2.normalize(hist, hist, 0, 255,
    cv2.NORM_MINMAX);
    self.hist = hist.reshape(-1)

    vis_roi = vis[y0:y1, x0:x1]
    cv2.bitwise_not(vis_roi, vis_roi)
    vis[mask == 0] = 0

if self.tracking_state == 1:
    self.selection = None

    # Compute the histogram back projection
    prob = cv2.calcBackProject([hsv], [0],
    self.hist, [0, 180], 1)

    prob &= mask
    term_crit = ( cv2.TERM_CRITERIA_EPS |
    cv2.TERM_CRITERIA_COUNT, 10, 1 )
```

```
        # Apply CAMShift on 'prob'
        track_box, self.track_window = cv2.CamShift(prob,
        self.track_window, term_crit)

        # Draw an ellipse around the object
        cv2.ellipse(vis, track_box, (0, 255, 0), 2)

    cv2.imshow('Object Tracker', vis)

    c = cv2.waitKey(5)
    if c == 27:
        break

  cv2.destroyAllWindows()

if __name__ == '__main__':
    ObjectTracker().start_tracking()
```

# Feature based tracking

Feature based tracking refers to tracking individual feature points across successive frames in the video. We use a technique called **optical flow** to track these features. Optical flow is one of the most popular techniques in computer vision. We choose a bunch of feature points and track them through the video stream.

When we detect the feature points, we compute the displacement vectors and show the motion of those keypoints between consecutive frames. These vectors are called motion vectors. There are many ways to do this, but the Lucas-Kanade method is perhaps the most popular of all these techniques. You can refer to their original paper at http://cseweb.ucsd.edu/classes/sp02/cse252/lucaskanade81.pdf. We start the process by extracting the feature points. For each feature point, we create 3x3 patches with the feature point in the center. The assumption here is that all the points within each patch will have a similar motion. We can adjust the size of this window depending on the problem at hand.

For each feature point in the current frame, we take the surrounding 3x3 patch as our reference point. For this patch, we look in its neighborhood in the previous frame to get the best match. This neighborhood is usually bigger than 3x3 because we want to get the patch that's closest to the patch under consideration. Now, the path from the center pixel of the matched patch in the previous frame to the center pixel of the patch under consideration in the current frame will become the motion vector. We do that for all the feature points and extract all the motion vectors.

Let's consider the following frame:

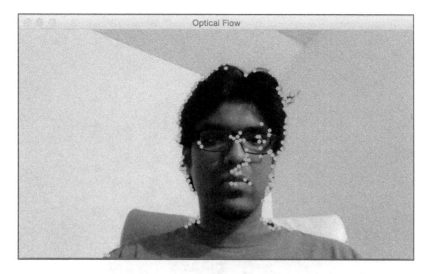

If I move in a horizontal direction, you will see the motion vectors in a horizontal direction:

If I move away from the webcam, you will see something like this:

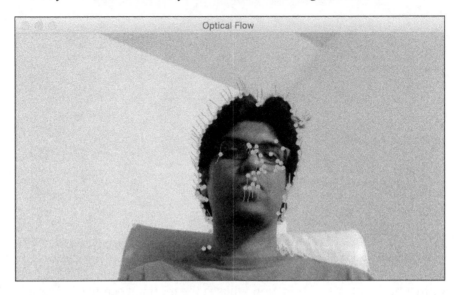

So, if you want to play around with it, you can let the user select a region of interest in the input video (like we did earlier). You can then extract feature points from this region of interest and track the object by drawing the bounding box. It will be a fun exercise!

Here is the code to perform optical flow based tracking:

```python
import cv2
import numpy as np

def start_tracking():
    # Capture the input frame
    cap = cv2.VideoCapture(0)

    # Downsampling factor for the image
    scaling_factor = 0.5

    # Number of frames to keep in the buffer when you
    # are tracking. If you increase this number,
    # feature points will have more "inertia"
    num_frames_to_track = 5

    # Skip every 'n' frames. This is just to increase the speed.
    num_frames_jump = 2
```

```
tracking_paths = []
frame_index = 0

# 'winSize' refers to the size of each patch. These patches
# are the smallest blocks on which we operate and track
# the feature points. You can read more about the parameters
# here: http://goo.gl/ulwqLk
tracking_params = dict(winSize  = (11, 11), maxLevel = 2,
        criteria = (cv2.TERM_CRITERIA_EPS |
        cv2.TERM_CRITERIA_COUNT, 10, 0.03))

# Iterate until the user presses the ESC key
while True:
    # read the input frame
    ret, frame = cap.read()

    # downsample the input frame
    frame = cv2.resize(frame, None, fx=scaling_factor,
            fy=scaling_factor, interpolation=cv2.INTER_AREA)

    frame_gray = cv2.cvtColor(frame, cv2.COLOR_BGR2GRAY)
    output_img = frame.copy()

    if len(tracking_paths) > 0:
        prev_img, current_img = prev_gray, frame_gray
        feature_points_0 = np.float32([tp[-1] for tp in
        tracking_paths]).reshape(-1, 1, 2)

        # Compute feature points using optical flow. You can
        # refer to the documentation to learn more about the
        # parameters here: http://goo.gl/t6P4SE
        feature_points_1, _, _ =
        cv2.calcOpticalFlowPyrLK(prev_img,
        current_img, feature_points_0,
                None, **tracking_params)
        feature_points_0_rev, _, _ =
        cv2.calcOpticalFlowPyrLK(current_img, prev_img,
        feature_points_1,
                None, **tracking_params)

        # Compute the difference of the feature points
        diff_feature_points = abs(feature_points_0-
        feature_points_0_rev).reshape(-1, 2).max(-1)
```

```
# threshold and keep the good points
good_points = diff_feature_points < 1

new_tracking_paths = []

for tp, (x, y), good_points_flag in
zip(tracking_paths,
            feature_points_1.reshape(-1, 2),
            good_points):
    if not good_points_flag:
        continue

    tp.append((x, y))

    # Using the queue structure i.e. first in,
    # first out
    if len(tp) > num_frames_to_track:
        del tp[0]

    new_tracking_paths.append(tp)

    # draw green circles on top of the output image
    cv2.circle(output_img, (x, y), 3, (0, 255, 0), -1)

tracking_paths = new_tracking_paths

# draw green lines on top of the output image
cv2.polylines(output_img, [np.int32(tp) for tp in
tracking_paths], False, (0, 150, 0))

# 'if' condition to skip every 'n'th frame
if not frame_index % num_frames_jump:
    mask = np.zeros_like(frame_gray)
    mask[:] = 255
    for x, y in [np.int32(tp[-1]) for tp in
    tracking_paths]:
        cv2.circle(mask, (x, y), 6, 0, -1)

    # Extract good features to track. You can learn more
    # about the parameters here: http://goo.gl/BI2Kml
    feature_points = cv2.goodFeaturesToTrack(frame_gray,
            mask = mask, maxCorners = 500,
            qualityLevel = 0.3,
            minDistance = 7, blockSize = 7)
```

```
    if feature_points is not None:
        for x, y in np.float32(feature_points).reshape
        (-1, 2):
            tracking_paths.append([(x, y)])

frame_index += 1
prev_gray = frame_gray

cv2.imshow('Optical Flow', output_img)

# Check if the user pressed the ESC key
c = cv2.waitKey(1)
if c == 27:
    break

if __name__ == '__main__':
    start_tracking()
    cv2.destroyAllWindows()
```

# Background subtraction

Background subtraction is very useful in video surveillance. Basically, background subtraction technique performs really well for cases where we have to detect moving objects in a static scene. As the name indicates, this algorithm works by detecting the background and subtracting it from the current frame to obtain the foreground, that is, moving objects. In order to detect moving objects, we need to build a model of the background first. This is not the same as frame differencing because we are actually modeling the background and using this model to detect moving objects. So, this performs much better than the simple frame differencing technique. This technique tries to detect static parts in the scene and then include it in the background model. So, it's an adaptive technique that can adjust according to the scene.

Let's consider the following image:

Now, as we gather more frames in this scene, every part of the image will gradually become a part of the background model. This is what we discussed earlier as well. If a scene is static, the model adapts itself to make sure the background model is updated. This is how it looks in the beginning:

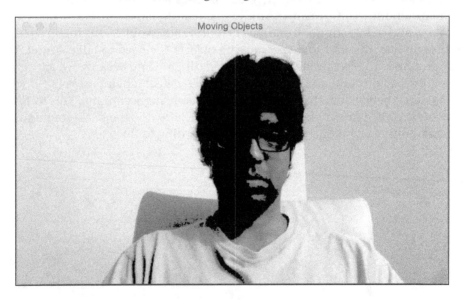

Notice how a part of my face has already become a part of the background model (the blackened region). The following screenshot shows what we'll see after a few seconds:

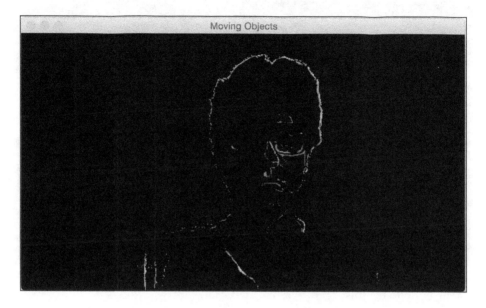

If we keep going, everything eventually becomes part of the background model:

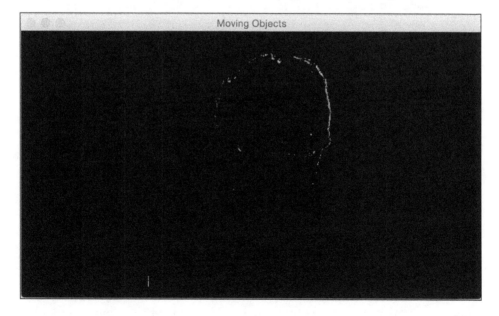

Now, if we introduce a new moving object, it will be detected clearly, as shown next:

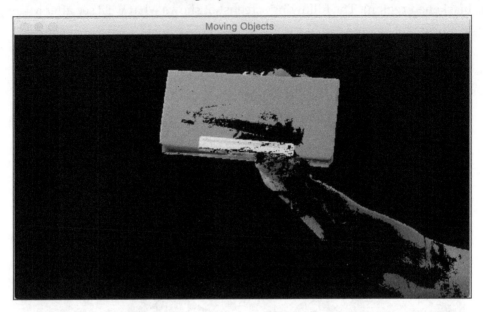

Here is the code to do this:

```python
import cv2
import numpy as np

# Capture the input frame
def get_frame(cap, scaling_factor=0.5):
    ret, frame = cap.read()

    # Resize the frame
    frame = cv2.resize(frame, None, fx=scaling_factor,
            fy=scaling_factor, interpolation=cv2.INTER_AREA)

    return frame

if __name__=='__main__':
    # Initialize the video capture object
    cap = cv2.VideoCapture(0)

    # Create the background subtractor object
    bgSubtractor = cv2.BackgroundSubtractorMOG()

    # This factor controls the learning rate of the algorithm.
    # The learning rate refers to the rate at which your model
```

```
# will learn about the background. Higher value for
# 'history' indicates a slower learning rate. You
# can play with this parameter to see how it affects
# the output.
history = 100

# Iterate until the user presses the ESC key
while True:
    frame = get_frame(cap, 0.5)

    # Apply the background subtraction model to the
    # input frame
    mask = bgSubtractor.apply(frame,
    learningRate=1.0/history)

    # Convert from grayscale to 3-channel RGB
    mask = cv2.cvtColor(mask, cv2.COLOR_GRAY2BGR)

    cv2.imshow('Input frame', frame)
    cv2.imshow('Moving Objects', mask & frame)

    # Check if the user pressed the ESC key
    c = cv2.waitKey(10)
    if c == 27:
        break

cap.release()
cv2.destroyAllWindows()
```

# Summary

In this chapter, we learned about object tracking. We learned how to get motion information using frame differencing, and how it can be limiting when we want to track different types of objects. We learned about colorspacethresholding and how it can be used to track colored objects. We discussed clustering techniques for object tracking and how we can build an interactive object tracker using the CAMShift algorithm. We discussed how to track features in a video and how we can use optical flow to achieve the same. We learned about background subtraction and how it can be used for video surveillance.

In the next chapter, we are going to discuss object recognition, and how we can build a visual search engine.

# 10
# Object Recognition

In this chapter, we are going to learn about object recognition and how we can use it to build a visual search engine. We will discuss feature detection, building feature vectors, and using machine learning to build a classifier. We will learn how to use these different blocks to build an object recognition system.

By the end of this chapter, you will know:

- What is the difference between object detection and object recognition
- What is a dense feature detector
- What is a visual dictionary
- How to build a feature vector
- What is supervised and unsupervised learning
- What are Support Vector Machines and how to use them to build a classifier
- How to recognize an object in an unknown image

## Object detection versus object recognition

Before we proceed, we need to understand what we are going to discuss in this chapter. You must have frequently heard the terms "object detection" and "object recognition", and they are often mistaken to be the same thing. There is a very distinct difference between the two.

Object detection refers to detecting the presence of a particular object in a given scene. We don't know what the object might be. For instance, we discussed face detection in *Chapter 4, Detecting and Tracking Different Body Parts*. During the discussion, we only detected whether or not a face is present in the given image. We didn't recognize the person! The reason we didn't recognize the person is because we didn't care about that in our discussion. Our goal was to find the location of the face in the given image. Commercial face recognition systems employ both face detection and face recognition to identify a person. First, we need to locate the face, and then, run the face recognizer on the cropped face.

Object recognition is the process of identifying an object in a given image. For instance, an object recognition system can tell you if a given image contains a dress or a pair of shoes. In fact, we can train an object recognition system to identify many different objects. The problem is that object recognition is a really difficult problem to solve. It has eluded computer vision researchers for decades now, and has become the holy grail of computer vision. Humans can identify a wide variety of objects very easily. We do it everyday and we do it effortlessly, but computers are unable to do it with that kind of accuracy.

Let's consider the following image of a latte cup:

An object detector will give you the following information:

Now, consider the following image of a teacup:

If you run it through an object detector, you will see the following result:

As you can see, the object detector detects the presence of the teacup, but nothing more than that. If you train an object recognizer, it will give you the following information, as shown in the image below:

If you consider the second image, it will give you the following information:

As you can see, a perfect object recognizer would give you all the information associated with that object. An object recognizer functions more accurately if it knows where the object is located. If you have a big image and the cup is a small part of it, then the object recognizer might not be able to recognize it. Hence, the first step is to detect the object and get the bounding box. Once we have that, we can run an object recognizer to extract more information.

# What is a dense feature detector?

In order to extract a meaningful amount of information from the images, we need to make sure our feature extractor extracts features from all the parts of a given image. Consider the following image:

If you extract features using a feature extractor, it will look like this:

If you use `Dense` detector, it will look like this:

We can control the density as well. Let's make it sparse:

By doing this, we can make sure that every single part in the image is processed. Here is the code to do it:

```
import cv2
import numpy as np

class DenseDetector(object):
    def __init__(self, step_size=20, feature_scale=40,
    img_bound=20):
        # Create a dense feature detector
        self.detector = cv2.FeatureDetector_create("Dense")

        # Initialize it with all the required parameters
        self.detector.setInt("initXyStep", step_size)
        self.detector.setInt("initFeatureScale", feature_scale)
        self.detector.setInt("initImgBound", img_bound)

    def detect(self, img):
        # Run feature detector on the input image
        return self.detector.detect(img)
```

```
if __name__=='__main__':
    input_image = cv2.imread(sys.argv[1])
    input_image_sift = np.copy(input_image)

    # Convert to grayscale
    gray_image = cv2.cvtColor(input_image, cv2.COLOR_BGR2GRAY)

    keypoints = DenseDetector(20,20,5).detect(input_image)

    # Draw keypoints on top of the input image
    input_image = cv2.drawKeypoints(input_image, keypoints,
            flags=cv2.DRAW_MATCHES_FLAGS_DRAW_RICH_KEYPOINTS)

    # Display the output image
    cv2.imshow('Dense feature detector', input_image)

    # Initialize SIFT object
    sift = cv2.SIFT()

    # Detect keypoints using SIFT
    keypoints = sift.detect(gray_image, None)

    # Draw SIFT keypoints on the input image
    input_image_sift = cv2.drawKeypoints(input_image_sift,
            keypoints,
            flags=cv2.DRAW_MATCHES_FLAGS_DRAW_RICH_KEYPOINTS)

    # Display the output image
    cv2.imshow('SIFT detector', input_image_sift)

    # Wait until user presses a key
    cv2.waitKey()
```

This gives us close control over the amount of information that gets extracted. When we use a SIFT detector, some parts of the image are neglected. This works well when we are dealing with the detection of prominent features, but when we are building an object recognizer, we need to evaluate all parts of the image. Hence, we use a dense detector and then extract features from those keypoints.

# What is a visual dictionary?

We will be using the **Bag of Words** model to build our object recognizer. Each image is represented as a histogram of visual words. These visual words are basically the **N** centroids built using all the keypoints extracted from training images. The pipeline is as shown in the image that follows:

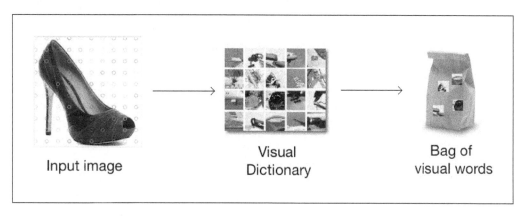

From each training image, we detect a set of keypoints and extract features for each of those keypoints. Every image will give rise to a different number of keypoints. In order to train a classifier, each image must be represented using a fixed length feature vector. This feature vector is nothing but a histogram, where each bin corresponds to a visual word.

When we extract all the features from all the keypoints in the training images, we perform K-Means clustering and extract N centroids. This N is the length of the feature vector of a given image. Each image will now be represented as a histogram, where each bin corresponds to one of the 'N' centroids. For simplicity, let's say that N is set to 4. Now, in a given image, we extract **K** keypoints. Out of these K keypoints, some of them will be closest to the first centroid, some of them will be closest to the second centroid, and so on. So, we build a histogram based on the closest centroid to each keypoint. This histogram becomes our feature vector. This process is called **vector quantization**.

To understand vector quantization, let's consider an example. Assume we have an image and we've extracted a certain number of feature points from it. Now our goal is to represent this image in the form of a feature vector. Consider the following image:

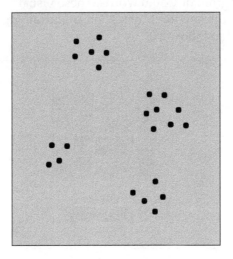

As you can see, we have 4 centroids. Bear in mind that the points shown in the figures represent the feature space and not the actual geometric locations of those feature points in the image. It is shown this way in the preceding figure so that it's easy to visualize. Points from many different geometric locations in an image can be close to each other in the feature space. Our goal is to represent this image as a histogram, where each bin corresponds to one of these centroids. This way, no matter how many feature points we extract from an image, it will always be converted to a fixed length feature vector. So, we "round off" each feature point to its nearest centroid, as shown in the next image:

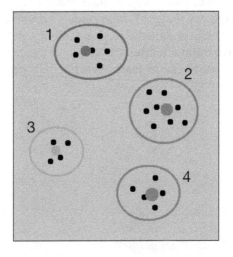

If you build a histogram for this image, it will look like this:

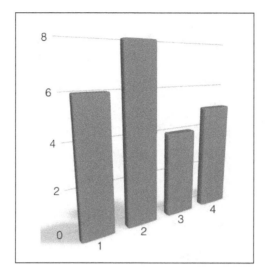

Now, if you consider a different image with a different distribution of feature points, it will look like this:

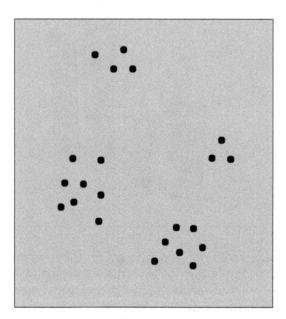

The clusters would look like the following:

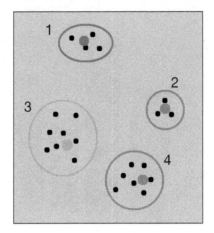

The histogram would look like this:

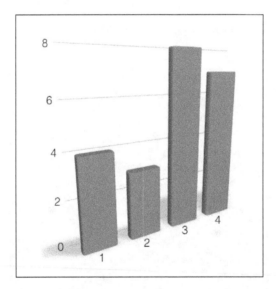

As you can see, the histograms are very different for the two images even though the points seem to be randomly distributed. This is a very powerful technique and it's widely used in computer vision and signal processing. There are many different ways to do this and the accuracy depends on how fine-grained you want it to be. If you increase the number of centroids, you will be able to represent the image better, thereby increasing the uniqueness of your feature vector. Having said that, it's important to mention that you cannot just keep increasing the number of centroids indefinitely. If you do that, it will become too noisy and lose its power.

# What is supervised and unsupervised learning?

If you are familiar with the basics of machine learning, you will certainly know what supervised and unsupervised learning is all about. To give a quick refresher, supervised learning refers to building a function based on labeled samples. For example, if we are building a system to separate dress images from footwear images, we first need to build a database and label it. We need to tell our algorithm what images correspond to dresses and what images correspond to footwear. Based on this data, the algorithm will learn how to identify dresses and footwear so that when an unknown image comes in, it can recognize what's inside that image.

Unsupervised learning is the opposite of what we just discussed. There is no labeled data available here. Let's say we have a bunch of images, and we just want to separate them into three groups. We don't know what the criteria will be. So, an unsupervised learning algorithm will try to separate the given set of data into 3 groups in the best possible way. The reason we are discussing this is because we will be using a combination of supervised and unsupervised learning to build our object recognition system.

# What are Support Vector Machines?

**Support Vector Machines (SVM)** are supervised learning models that are very popular in the realm of machine learning. SVMs are really good at analyzing labeled data and detecting patterns. Given a bunch of data points and the associated labels, SVMs will build the separating hyperplanes in the best possible way.
Wait a minute, what are "hyperplanes"? To understand that, let's consider the following figure:

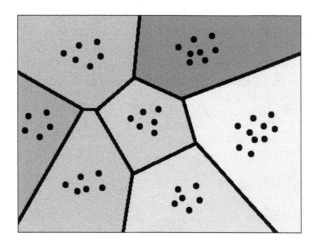

As you can see, the points are being separated by line boundaries that are equidistant from the points. This is easy to visualize in 2 dimensions. If it were in 3 dimensions, the separators would be planes. When we build features for images, the length of the feature vectors is usually in the six-digit range. So, when we go to such a high dimensional space, the equivalent of "lines" would be hyperplanes. Once the hyperplanes are formulated, we use this mathematical model to classify unknown data, based on where it falls on this map.

## What if we cannot separate the data with simple straight lines?

There is something called the **kernel trick** that we use in SVMs. Consider the following image:

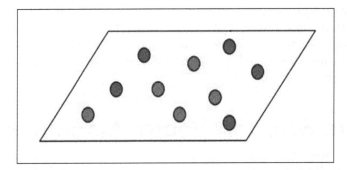

As we can see, we cannot draw a simple straight line to separate the red points from the blue points. Coming up with a nice curvy boundary that will satisfy all the points is prohibitively expensive. SVMs are really good at drawing "straight lines". So, what's our answer here? The good thing about SVMs is that they can draw these "straight lines" in any number of dimensions. So technically, if you project these points into a high dimensional space, where they can separated by a simple hyperplane, SVMs will come up with an exact boundary. Once we have that boundary, we can project it back to the original space. The projection of this hyperplane on our original lower dimensional space looks curvy, as we can see in the next figure:

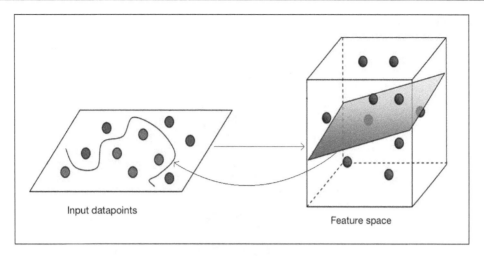

Input datapoints

Feature space

The topic of SVMs is really deep and we will not be able to discuss it in detail here. If you are really interested, there is a ton of material available online. You can go through a simple tutorial to understand it better.

# How do we actually implement this?

We have now arrived at the core. The discussion up until now was necessary because it gives you the background required to build an object recognition system. Now, let's build an object recognizer that can recognize whether the given image contains a dress, a pair of shoes, or a bag. We can easily extend this system to detect any number of items. We are starting with three distinct items so that you can start experimenting with it later.

Before we start, we need to make sure that we have a set of training images. There are many databases available online where the images are already arranged into groups. Caltech256 is perhaps one of the most popular databases for object recognition. You can download it from `http://www.vision.caltech.edu/Image_Datasets/Caltech256`. Create a folder called `images` and create three subfolders inside it, that is, `dress`, `footwear`, and `bag`. Inside each of those subfolders, add 20 images corresponding to that item. You can just download these images from the internet, but make sure those images have a clean background.

For example, a dress image would like this:

A footwear image would look like this:

A bag image would look like this:

Now that we have 60 training images, we are ready to start. As a side note, object recognition systems actually need tens of thousands of training images in order to perform well in the real world. Since we are building an object recognizer to detect 3 types of objects, we will take only 20 training images per object. Adding more training images will increase the accuracy and robustness of our system.

The first step here is to extract feature vectors from all the training images and build the visual dictionary (also known as codebook). Here is the code:

```
import os
import sys
import argparse
import cPickle as pickle
import json

import cv2
import numpy as np
from sklearn.cluster import KMeans
```

```
def build_arg_parser():
    parser = argparse.ArgumentParser(description='Creates features
    for given images')
    parser.add_argument("--samples", dest="cls", nargs="+",
    action="append",
            required=True, help="Folders containing the training
            images. \
            The first element needs to be the class label.")
    parser.add_argument("--codebook-file", dest='codebook_file',
    required=True,
            help="Base file name to store the codebook")
    parser.add_argument("--feature-map-file",
    dest='feature_map_file', required=True,
            help="Base file name to store the feature map")

    return parser

# Loading the images from the input folder
def load_input_map(label, input_folder):
    combined_data = []

    if not os.path.isdir(input_folder):
        raise IOError("The folder " + input_folder + " doesn't
        exist")

    # Parse the input folder and assign the  labels
    for root, dirs, files in os.walk(input_folder):
        for filename in (x for x in files if x.endswith('.jpg')):
            combined_data.append({'label': label, 'image':
            os.path.join(root, filename)})

    return combined_data

class FeatureExtractor(object):
    def extract_image_features(self, img):
        # Dense feature detector
        kps = DenseDetector().detect(img)

        # SIFT feature extractor
        kps, fvs = SIFTExtractor().compute(img, kps)

        return fvs
```

```
        # Extract the centroids from the feature points
        def get_centroids(self, input_map, num_samples_to_fit=10):
            kps_all = []

            count = 0
            cur_label = ''
            for item in input_map:
                if count >= num_samples_to_fit:
                    if cur_label != item['label']:
                        count = 0
                    else:
                        continue

                count += 1

                if count == num_samples_to_fit:
                    print "Built centroids for", item['label']

                cur_label = item['label']
                img = cv2.imread(item['image'])
                img = resize_to_size(img, 150)

                num_dims = 128
                fvs = self.extract_image_features(img)
                kps_all.extend(fvs)

            kmeans, centroids = Quantizer().quantize(kps_all)
            return kmeans, centroids

        def get_feature_vector(self, img, kmeans, centroids):
            return Quantizer().get_feature_vector(img, kmeans,
            centroids)

    def extract_feature_map(input_map, kmeans, centroids):
        feature_map = []

        for item in input_map:
            temp_dict = {}
            temp_dict['label'] = item['label']

            print "Extracting features for", item['image']
            img = cv2.imread(item['image'])
            img = resize_to_size(img, 150)
```

```
                 temp_dict['feature_vector'] =
                 FeatureExtractor().get_feature_vector(
                         img, kmeans, centroids)

                 if temp_dict['feature_vector'] is not None:
                     feature_map.append(temp_dict)

        return feature_map

# Vector quantization
class Quantizer(object):
    def __init__(self, num_clusters=32):
        self.num_dims = 128
        self.extractor = SIFTExtractor()
        self.num_clusters = num_clusters
        self.num_retries = 10

    def quantize(self, datapoints):
        # Create KMeans object
        kmeans = KMeans(self.num_clusters,
                        n_init=max(self.num_retries, 1),
                        max_iter=10, tol=1.0)

        # Run KMeans on the datapoints
        res = kmeans.fit(datapoints)

        # Extract the centroids of those clusters
        centroids = res.cluster_centers_

        return kmeans, centroids

    def normalize(self, input_data):
        sum_input = np.sum(input_data)
        if sum_input > 0:
            return input_data / sum_input
        else:
            return input_data

    # Extract feature vector from the image
    def get_feature_vector(self, img, kmeans, centroids):
        kps = DenseDetector().detect(img)
        kps, fvs = self.extractor.compute(img, kps)
        labels = kmeans.predict(fvs)
```

```
            fv = np.zeros(self.num_clusters)

            for i, item in enumerate(fvs):
                fv[labels[i]] += 1

            fv_image = np.reshape(fv, ((1, fv.shape[0])))
            return self.normalize(fv_image)

class DenseDetector(object):
    def __init__(self, step_size=20, feature_scale=40,
    img_bound=20):
        self.detector = cv2.FeatureDetector_create("Dense")
        self.detector.setInt("initXyStep", step_size)
        self.detector.setInt("initFeatureScale", feature_scale)
        self.detector.setInt("initImgBound", img_bound)

    def detect(self, img):
        return self.detector.detect(img)

class SIFTExtractor(object):
    def compute(self, image, kps):
        if image is None:
            print "Not a valid image"
            raise TypeError

        gray_image = cv2.cvtColor(image, cv2.COLOR_BGR2GRAY)
        kps, des = cv2.SIFT().compute(gray_image, kps)
        return kps, des

# Resize the shorter dimension to 'new_size'
# while maintaining the aspect ratio
def resize_to_size(input_image, new_size=150):
    h, w = input_image.shape[0], input_image.shape[1]
    ds_factor = new_size / float(h)

    if w < h:
        ds_factor = new_size / float(w)

    new_size = (int(w * ds_factor), int(h * ds_factor))
    return cv2.resize(input_image, new_size)

if __name__=='__main__':
    args = build_arg_parser().parse_args()
```

```
input_map = []
for cls in args.cls:

    assert len(cls) >= 2, "Format for classes is `<label>
    file`"
    label = cls[0]
    input_map += load_input_map(label, cls[1])

# Building the codebook
print "===== Building codebook ====="
kmeans, centroids = FeatureExtractor().get_centroids(input_map)
if args.codebook_file:
    with open(args.codebook_file, 'w') as f:
        pickle.dump((kmeans, centroids), f)

# Input data and labels
print "===== Building feature map ====="
feature_map = extract_feature_map(input_map, kmeans,
centroids)
if args.feature_map_file:
    with open(args.feature_map_file, 'w') as f:
        pickle.dump(feature_map, f)
```

# What happened inside the code?

The first thing we need to do is extract the centroids. This is how we are going to build our visual dictionary. The get_centroids method in the FeatureExtractor class is designed to do this. We keep collecting the image features extracted from keypoints until we have a sufficient number of them. Since we are using a dense detector, 10 images should be sufficient. The reason we are just taking 10 images is because they will give rise to a large number of features. The centroids will not change much even if you add more feature points.

Once we've extracted the centroids, we are ready to move on to the next step of feature extraction. The set of centroids is our visual dictionary. The function, extract_feature_map, will extract a feature vector from each image and associate it with the corresponding label. The reason we do this is because we need this mapping to train our classifier. We need a set of datapoints, and each datapoint should be associated with a label. So, we start from an image, extract the feature vector, and then associate it with the corresponding label (like bag, dress, or footwear).

The Quantizer class is designed to achieve vector quantization and build the feature vector. For each keypoint extracted from the image, the get_feature_vector method finds the closest visual word in our dictionary. By doing this, we end up building a histogram based on our visual dictionary. Each image is now represented as a combination from a set of visual words. Hence the name, **Bag of Words**.

The next step is to train the classifier using these features. Here is the code:

```python
import os
import sys
import argparse

import cPickle as pickle
import numpy as np
from sklearn.multiclass import OneVsOneClassifier
from sklearn.svm import LinearSVC
from sklearn import preprocessing

def build_arg_parser():
    parser = argparse.ArgumentParser(description='Trains the
    classifier models')
    parser.add_argument("--feature-map-file",
    dest="feature_map_file", required=True,
            help="Input pickle file containing the feature map")
    parser.add_argument("--svm-file", dest="svm_file",
    required=False,
            help="Output file where the pickled SVM model will be
            stored")
    return parser

# To train the classifier
class ClassifierTrainer(object):
    def __init__(self, X, label_words):
        # Encoding the labels (words to numbers)
        self.le = preprocessing.LabelEncoder()

        # Initialize One vs One Classifier using a linear kernel
        self.clf = OneVsOneClassifier(LinearSVC(random_state=0))

        y = self._encodeLabels(label_words)
        X = np.asarray(X)
        self.clf.fit(X, y)
```

```python
        # Predict the output class for the input datapoint
        def _fit(self, X):
            X = np.asarray(X)
            return self.clf.predict(X)

        # Encode the labels (convert words to numbers)
        def _encodeLabels(self, labels_words):
            self.le.fit(labels_words)
            return np.array(self.le.transform(labels_words),
            dtype=np.float32)

        # Classify the input datapoint
        def classify(self, X):
            labels_nums = self._fit(X)
            labels_words = self.le.inverse_transform([int(x) for x in
            labels_nums])
            return labels_words

if __name__=='__main__':
    args = build_arg_parser().parse_args()
    feature_map_file = args.feature_map_file
    svm_file = args.svm_file

    # Load the feature map
    with open(feature_map_file, 'r') as f:
        feature_map = pickle.load(f)

    # Extract feature vectors and the labels
    labels_words = [x['label'] for x in feature_map]

    # Here, 0 refers to the first element in the
    # feature_map, and 1 refers to the second
    # element in the shape vector of that element
    # (which gives us the size)
    dim_size = feature_map[0]['feature_vector'].shape[1]

    X = [np.reshape(x['feature_vector'], (dim_size,)) for x in
    feature_map]

    # Train the SVM
    svm = ClassifierTrainer(X, labels_words)
    if args.svm_file:
        with open(args.svm_file, 'w') as f:
            pickle.dump(svm, f)
```

# How did we build the trainer?

We use the `scikit-learn` package to build the SVM model. You can install it, as shown next:

```
$ pip install scikit-learn
```

We start with labeled data and feed it to the `OneVsOneClassifier` method. We have a `classify` method that classifies an input image and associates a label with it.

Let's give this a trial run, shall we? Make sure you have a folder called `images`, where you have the training images for the three classes. Create a folder called `models`, where the learning models will be stored. Run the following commands on your terminal to create the features and train the classifier:

```
$ python create_features.py --samples bag images/bag/ --samples dress
images/dress/ --samples footwear images/footwear/ --codebook-file
models/codebook.pkl --feature-map-file models/feature_map.pkl
```

```
$ python training.py --feature-map-file models/feature_map.pkl
--svm-file models/svm.pkl
```

Now that the classifier has been trained, we just need a module to classify the input image and detect the object inside. Here is the code to do it:

```python
import os
import sys
import argparse
import cPickle as pickle

import cv2
import numpy as np

import create_features as cf
from training import ClassifierTrainer

def build_arg_parser():
    parser = argparse.ArgumentParser(description='Extracts
    features \
            from each line and classifies the data')
    parser.add_argument("--input-image", dest="input_image",
    required=True,
            help="Input image to be classified")
    parser.add_argument("--svm-file", dest="svm_file",
    required=True,
            help="File containing the trained SVM model")
    parser.add_argument("--codebook-file", dest="codebook_file",
```

```
                    required=True, help="File containing the codebook")
        return parser

    # Classifying an image
    class ImageClassifier(object):
        def __init__(self, svm_file, codebook_file):
            # Load the SVM classifier
            with open(svm_file, 'r') as f:
                self.svm = pickle.load(f)

            # Load the codebook
            with open(codebook_file, 'r') as f:
                self.kmeans, self.centroids = pickle.load(f)

        # Method to get the output image tag
        def getImageTag(self, img):
            # Resize the input image
            img = cf.resize_to_size(img)

            # Extract the feature vector
            feature_vector =
            cf.FeatureExtractor().get_feature_vector(img, self.kmeans,
            self.centroids)

            # Classify the feature vector and get the output tag
            image_tag = self.svm.classify(feature_vector)

            return image_tag

    if __name__=='__main__':
        args = build_arg_parser().parse_args()
        svm_file = args.svm_file
        codebook_file = args.codebook_file
        input_image = cv2.imread(args.input_image)

        print "Output class:", ImageClassifier(svm_file,
        codebook_file).getImageTag(input_image)
```

We are all set! We just extract the `feature` vector from the input image and use it as the input argument to the classifier. Let's go ahead and see if this works. Download a random footwear image from the internet and make sure it has a clean background. Run the following command by replacing `new_image.jpg` with the right filename:

```
$ python classify_data.py --input-image new_image.jpg --svm-file
models/svm.pkl --codebook-file models/codebook.pkl
```

We can use the same technique to build a visual search engine. A visual search engine looks at the input image and shows a bunch of images that are similar to it. We can reuse the object recognition framework to build this. Extract the feature vector from the input image, and compare it with all the feature vectors in the training dataset. Pick out the top matches and display the results. This is a simple way of doing things!

In the real world, we have to deal with billions of images. So, you cannot afford to search through every single image before you display the output. There are a lot of algorithms that are used to make sure that this is efficient and fast in the real world. Deep Learning is being used extensively in this field and it has shown a lot of promise in recent years. It is a branch of machine learning that focuses on learning optimal representation of data, so that it becomes easier for the machines to *learn* new tasks. You can learn more about it at `http://deeplearning.net`

# Summary

In this chapter, we learned how to build an object recognition system. The differences between object detection and object recognition were discussed in detail. We learned about the dense feature detector, visual dictionary, vector quantization, and how to use these concepts to build a feature vector. The concepts of supervised and unsupervised learning were discussed. We talked about Support Vector Machines and how we can use them to build a classifier. We learned how to recognize an object in an unknown image, and how we can extend that concept to build a visual search engine.

In the next chapter, we are going to discuss stereo imaging and 3D reconstruction. We will talk about how we can build a depth map and extract the 3D information from a given scene.

# 11
# Stereo Vision and 3D Reconstruction

In this chapter, we are going to learn about stereo vision and how we can reconstruct the 3D map of a scene. We will discuss epipolar geometry, depth maps, and 3D reconstruction. We will learn how to extract 3D information from stereo images and build a point cloud.

By the end of this chapter, you will know:

- What is stereo correspondence
- What is epipolar geometry
- What is a depth map
- How to extract 3D information
- How to build and visualize the 3D map of a given scene

## What is stereo correspondence?

When we capture images, we project the 3D world around us on a 2D image plane. So technically, we only have 2D information when we capture those photos. Since all the objects in that scene are projected onto a flat 2D plane, the depth information is lost. We have no way of knowing how far an object is from the camera or how the objects are positioned with respect to each other in the 3D space. This is where stereo vision comes into the picture.

Humans are very good at inferring depth information from the real world. The reason is that we have two eyes positioned a couple of inches from each other. Each eye acts as a camera and we capture two images of the same scene from two different viewpoints, that is, one image each using the left and right eyes. So, our brain takes these two images and builds a 3D map using stereo vision. This is what we want to achieve using stereo vision algorithms. We can capture two photos of the same scene using different viewpoints, and then match the corresponding points to obtain the depth map of the scene.

Let's consider the following image:

Now, if we capture the same scene from a different angle, it will look like this:

As you can see, there is a large amount of movement in the positions of the objects in the image. If you consider the pixel coordinates, the values of the initial position and final position will differ by a large amount in these two images. Consider the following image:

If we consider the same line of distance in the second image, it will look like this:

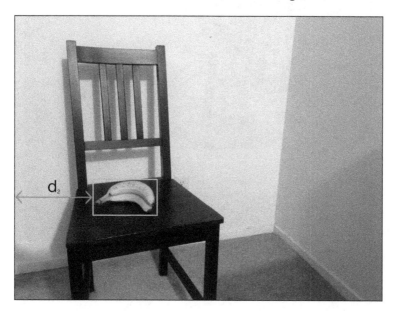

The difference between **d1** and **d2** is large. Now, let's bring the box closer to the camera:

Now, let's move the camera by the same amount as we did earlier, and capture the same scene from this angle:

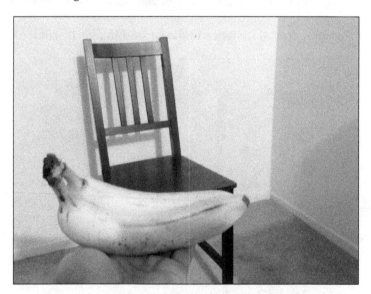

As you can see, the movement between the positions of the objects is not much. If you consider the pixel coordinates, you will see that the values are close to each other. The distance in the first image would be:

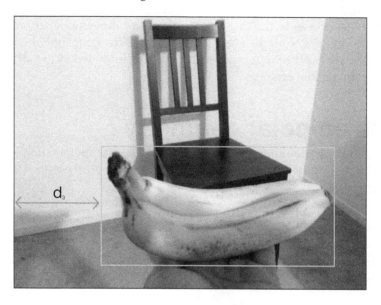

If we consider the same line of distance in the second image, it will be as shown in the following image:

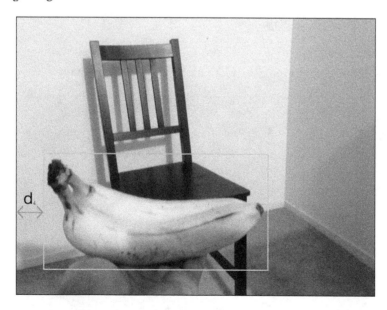

The difference between **d3** and **d4** is small. We can say that the absolute difference between **d1** and **d2** is greater than the absolute difference between **d3** and **d4**. Even though the camera moved by the same amount, there is a big difference between the apparent distances between the initial and final positions. This happens because we can bring the object closer to the camera; the apparent movement decreases when you capture two images from different angles. This is the concept behind stereo correspondence: we capture two images and use this knowledge to extract the depth information from a given scene.

# What is epipolar geometry?

Before discussing epipolar geometry, let's discuss what happens when we capture two images of the same scene from two different viewpoints. Consider the following figure:

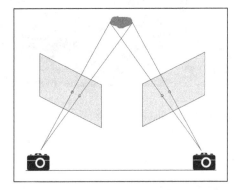

Let's see how it happens in real life. Consider the following image:

Now, let's capture the same scene from a different viewpoint:

Our goal is to match the keypoints in these two images to extract the scene information. The way we do this is by extracting a matrix that can associate the corresponding points between two stereo images. This is called the **fundamental matrix**.

As we saw in the camera figure earlier, we can draw lines to see where they meet. These lines are called **epipolar lines**. The point at which the epipolar lines converge is called epipole. If you match the keypoints using SIFT, and draw the lines towards the meeting point on the left image, it will look like this:

Following are the matching feature points in the right image:

The lines are epipolar lines. If you take the second image as the reference, they will appear as shown in the next image:

Following are the matching feature points in the first image:

It's important to understand epipolar geometry and how we draw these lines. If two frames are positioned in 3D, then each epipolar line between the two frames must intersect the corresponding feature in each frame and each of the camera origins. This can be used to estimate the pose of the cameras with respect to the 3D environment. We will use this information later on, to extract 3D information from the scene. Let's take a look at the code:

```python
import argparse

import cv2
import numpy as np

def build_arg_parser():
    parser = argparse.ArgumentParser(description='Find fundamental matrix \
            using the two input stereo images and draw epipolar
            lines')
    parser.add_argument("--img-left", dest="img_left", required=True,
            help="Image captured from the left view")
    parser.add_argument("--img-right", dest="img_right", required=True,
            help="Image captured from the right view")
    parser.add_argument("--feature-type", dest="feature_type",
```

```
                    required=True, help="Feature extractor that will be
                    used; can be either 'sift' or 'surf'")
        return parser

    def draw_lines(img_left, img_right, lines, pts_left, pts_right):
        h,w = img_left.shape
        img_left = cv2.cvtColor(img_left, cv2.COLOR_GRAY2BGR)
        img_right = cv2.cvtColor(img_right, cv2.COLOR_GRAY2BGR)

        for line, pt_left, pt_right in zip(lines, pts_left,
        pts_right):
            x_start,y_start = map(int, [0, -line[2]/line[1] ])
            x_end,y_end = map(int, [w, -(line[2]+line[0]*w)/line[1] ])
            color = tuple(np.random.randint(0,255,2).tolist())
            cv2.line(img_left, (x_start,y_start), (x_end,y_end),
            color,1)
            cv2.circle(img_left, tuple(pt_left), 5, color, -1)
            cv2.circle(img_right, tuple(pt_right), 5, color, -1)

        return img_left, img_right

    def get_descriptors(gray_image, feature_type):
        if feature_type == 'surf':
            feature_extractor = cv2.SURF()

        elif feature_type == 'sift':
            feature_extractor = cv2.SIFT()

        else:
            raise TypeError("Invalid feature type; should be either
            'surf' or 'sift'")

        keypoints, descriptors = feature_extractor.detectAndCompute(gray_
    image, None)
        return keypoints, descriptors

    if __name__=='__main__':
        args = build_arg_parser().parse_args()
        img_left = cv2.imread(args.img_left,0)  # left image
        img_right = cv2.imread(args.img_right,0)  # right image
        feature_type = args.feature_type

        if feature_type not in ['sift', 'surf']:
```

```
    raise TypeError("Invalid feature type; has to be either
    'sift' or 'surf'")

scaling_factor = 1.0
img_left = cv2.resize(img_left, None, fx=scaling_factor,
            fy=scaling_factor, interpolation=cv2.INTER_AREA)
img_right = cv2.resize(img_right, None, fx=scaling_factor,
            fy=scaling_factor, interpolation=cv2.INTER_AREA)

kps_left, des_left = get_descriptors(img_left, feature_type)
kps_right, des_right = get_descriptors(img_right, feature_type)

# FLANN parameters
FLANN_INDEX_KDTREE = 0
index_params = dict(algorithm = FLANN_INDEX_KDTREE, trees = 5)
search_params = dict(checks=50)

# Get the matches based on the descriptors
flann = cv2.FlannBasedMatcher(index_params, search_params)
matches = flann.knnMatch(des_left, des_right, k=2)

pts_left_image = []
pts_right_image = []

# ratio test to retain only the good matches
for i,(m,n) in enumerate(matches):
    if m.distance < 0.7*n.distance:
        pts_left_image.append(kps_left[m.queryIdx].pt)
        pts_right_image.append(kps_right[m.trainIdx].pt)

pts_left_image = np.float32(pts_left_image)
pts_right_image = np.float32(pts_right_image)
F, mask = cv2.findFundamentalMat(pts_left_image,
pts_right_image, cv2.FM_LMEDS)

# Selecting only the inliers
pts_left_image = pts_left_image[mask.ravel()==1]
pts_right_image = pts_right_image[mask.ravel()==1]

# Drawing the lines on left image and the corresponding feature
points on the right image
    lines1 = cv2.computeCorrespondEpilines
    (pts_right_image.reshape(-1,1,2), 2, F)
    lines1 = lines1.reshape(-1,3)
```

```
    img_left_lines, img_right_pts = draw_lines(img_left,
    img_right, lines1, pts_left_image, pts_right_image)

    # Drawing the lines on right image and the corresponding feature
points on the left image
    lines2 = cv2.computeCorrespondEpilines
    (pts_left_image.reshape(-1,1,2), 1,F)
    lines2 = lines2.reshape(-1,3)
    img_right_lines, img_left_pts = draw_lines(img_right,
    img_left, lines2, pts_right_image, pts_left_image)

    cv2.imshow('Epi lines on left image', img_left_lines)
    cv2.imshow('Feature points on right image', img_right_pts)
    cv2.imshow('Epi lines on right image', img_right_lines)
    cv2.imshow('Feature points on left image', img_left_pts)
    cv2.waitKey()
    cv2.destroyAllWindows()
```

Let's see what happens if we use the **SURF** feature extractor. The lines in the left image will look like this:

Following are the matching feature points in the right image:

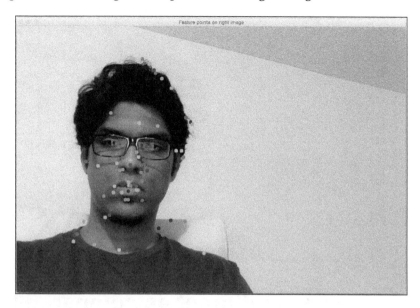

If you take the second image as the reference, you will see something like the following image:

These are the matching feature points in the first image:

# Why are the lines different as compared to SIFT?

SURF detects a different set of feature points, so the corresponding epipolar lines differ as well. As you can see in the images, there are more feature points detected when we use SURF. Since we have more information than before, the corresponding epipolar lines will also change accordingly.

# Building the 3D map

Now that we are familiar with epipolar geometry, let's see how to use it to build a 3D map based on stereo images. Let's consider the following figure:

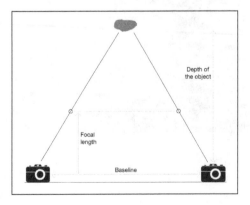

The first step is to extract the disparity map between the two images. If you look at the figure, as we go closer to the object from the cameras along the connecting lines, the distance decreases between the points. Using this information, we can infer the distance of each point from the camera. This is called a depth map. Once we find the matching points between the two images, we can find the disparity by using epipolar lines to impose epipolar constraints.

Let's consider the following image:

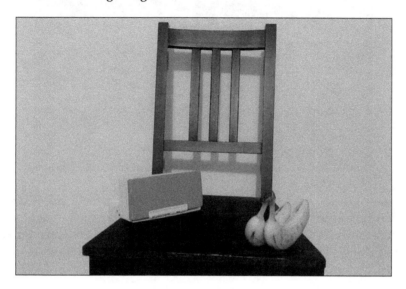

If we capture the same scene from a different position, we get the following image:

If we reconstruct the 3D map, it will look like this:

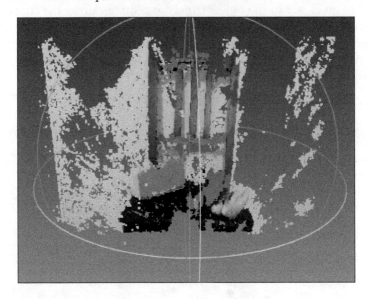

Bear in mind that these images were not captured using perfectly aligned stereo cameras. That's the reason the 3D map looks so noisy! This is just to demonstrate how we can reconstruct the real world using stereo images. Let's consider an image pair captured using stereo cameras that are properly aligned. Following is the left view image:

Next is the corresponding right view image:

If you extract the depth information and build the 3D map, it will look like this:

Let's rotate it to see if the depth is right for the different objects in the scene:

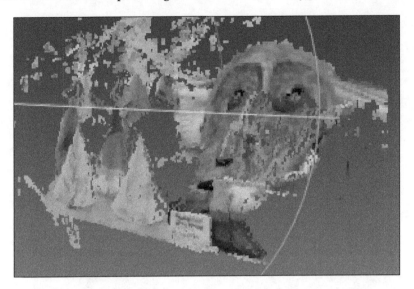

You need a software called **MeshLab** to visualize the 3D scene. We'll discuss about it soon. As we can see in the preceding images, the items are correctly aligned according to their distance from the camera. We can intuitively see that they are arranged in the right way, including the tilted position of the mask. We can use this technique to build many interesting things.

Let's see how to do it in OpenCV-Python:

```python
import argparse

import cv2
import numpy as np

def build_arg_parser():
    parser = argparse.ArgumentParser(description='Reconstruct the
    3D map from \
            the two input stereo images. Output will be saved in
            \'output.ply\'')
    parser.add_argument("--image-left", dest="image_left",
    required=True,
            help="Input image captured from the left")
    parser.add_argument("--image-right", dest="image_right",
    required=True,
            help="Input image captured from the right")
    parser.add_argument("--output-file", dest="output_file",
    required=True,
```

```
                  help="Output filename (without the extension) where
                  the point cloud will be saved")
        return parser

def create_output(vertices, colors, filename):
    colors = colors.reshape(-1, 3)
    vertices = np.hstack([vertices.reshape(-1,3), colors])

    ply_header = '''ply
        format ascii 1.0
        element vertex %(vert_num)d
        property float x
        property float y
        property float z
        property uchar red
        property uchar green
        property uchar blue
        end_header
    '''

    with open(filename, 'w') as f:
        f.write(ply_header % dict(vert_num=len(vertices)))
        np.savetxt(f, vertices, '%f %f %f %d %d %d')

if __name__ == '__main__':
    args = build_arg_parser().parse_args()
    image_left = cv2.imread(args.image_left)
    image_right = cv2.imread(args.image_right)
    output_file = args.output_file + '.ply'

    if image_left.shape[0] != image_right.shape[0] or \
            image_left.shape[1] != image_right.shape[1]:
        raise TypeError("Input images must be of the same size")

    # downscale images for faster processing
    image_left = cv2.pyrDown(image_left)
    image_right = cv2.pyrDown(image_right)

    # disparity range is tuned for 'aloe' image pair
    win_size = 1
    min_disp = 16
    max_disp = min_disp * 9
    num_disp = max_disp - min_disp   # Needs to be divisible by 16
    stereo = cv2.StereoSGBM(minDisparity = min_disp,
```

```
            numDisparities = num_disp,
            SADWindowSize = win_size,
            uniquenessRatio = 10,
            speckleWindowSize = 100,
            speckleRange = 32,
            disp12MaxDiff = 1,
            P1 = 8*3*win_size**2,
            P2 = 32*3*win_size**2,
            fullDP = True
        )

    print "\nComputing the disparity map ..."
    disparity_map = stereo.compute(image_left,
image_right).astype(np.float32) / 16.0

    print "\nGenerating the 3D map ..."
    h, w = image_left.shape[:2]
    focal_length = 0.8*w

    # Perspective transformation matrix
    Q = np.float32([[1, 0, 0, -w/2.0],
                    [0,-1, 0,  h/2.0],
                    [0, 0, 0, -focal_length],
                    [0, 0, 1, 0]])

    points_3D = cv2.reprojectImageTo3D(disparity_map, Q)
    colors = cv2.cvtColor(image_left, cv2.COLOR_BGR2RGB)
    mask_map = disparity_map > disparity_map.min()
    output_points = points_3D[mask_map]
    output_colors = colors[mask_map]

    print "\nCreating the output file ...\n"
    create_output(output_points, output_colors, output_file)
```

To visualize the output, you need to download MeshLab from `http://meshlab.sourceforge.net`

Just open the `output.ply` file using MeshLab and you'll see the 3D image. You can rotate it to get a complete 3D view of the reconstructed scene. Some of the alternatives to MeshLab are Sketchup on OS X and Windows, and Blender on Linux.

# Summary

In this chapter, we learned about stereo vision and 3D reconstruction. We discussed how to extract the fundamental matrix using different feature extractors. We learned how to generate the disparity map between two images, and use it to reconstruct the 3D map of a given scene.

In the next chapter, we are going to discuss augmented reality, and how we can build a cool application where we overlay graphics on top of real world objects in a live video.

# 12
# Augmented Reality

In this chapter, you are going to learn about augmented reality and how you can use it to build cool applications. We will discuss pose estimation and plane tracking. You will learn how to map the coordinates from 2D to 3D, and how we can overlay graphics on top of a live video.

By the end of this chapter, you will know:

- What is the premise of augmented reality
- What is pose estimation
- How to track a planar object
- How to map coordinates from 3D to 2D
- How to overlay graphics on top of a video in real time

## What is the premise of augmented reality?

Before we jump into all the fun stuff, let's understand what augmented reality means. You would have probably seen the term "augmented reality" being used in a variety of contexts. So, we should understand the premise of augmented reality before we start discussing the implementation details. Augmented Reality refers to the superposition of computer-generated input such as imagery, sounds, graphics, and text on top of the real world.

Augmented reality tries to blur the line between what's real and what's computer-generated by seamlessly merging the information and enhancing what we see and feel. It is actually closely related to a concept called mediated reality where a computer modifies our view of the reality. As a result of this, the technology works by enhancing our current perception of reality. Now the challenge here is to make it look seamless to the user. It's easy to just overlay something on top of the input video, but we need to make it look like it is part of the video. The user should feel that the computer-generated input is closely following the real world. This is what we want to achieve when we build an augmented reality system.

Computer vision research in this context explores how we can apply computer-generated imagery to live video streams so that we can enhance the perception of the real world. Augmented reality technology has a wide variety of applications including, but not limited to, head-mounted displays, automobiles, data visualization, gaming, construction, and so on. Now that we have powerful smartphones and smarter machines, we can build high-end augmented reality applications with ease.

# What does an augmented reality system look like?

Let's consider the following figure:

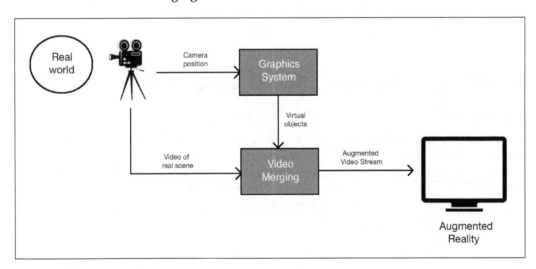

As we can see here, the camera captures the real world video to get the reference point. The graphics system generates the virtual objects that need to be overlaid on top of the video. Now the video-merging block is where all the magic happens. This block should be smart enough to understand how to overlay the virtual objects on top of the real world in the best way possible.

# Geometric transformations for augmented reality

The outcome of augmented reality is amazing, but there are a lot of mathematical things going on underneath. Augmented reality utilizes a lot of geometric transformations and the associated mathematical functions to make sure everything looks seamless. When talking about a live video for augmented reality, we need to precisely register the virtual objects on top of the real world. To understand it better, let's think of it as an alignment of two cameras—the real one through which we see the world, and the virtual one that projects the computer generated graphical objects.

In order to build an augmented reality system, the following geometric transformations need to be established:

- **Object-to-scene**: This transformation refers to transforming the 3D coordinates of a virtual object and expressing them in the coordinate frame of our real-world scene. This ensures that we are positioning the virtual object in the right location.

- **Scene-to-camera**: This transformation refers to the pose of the camera in the real world. By "pose", we mean the orientation and location of the camera. We need to estimate the point of view of the camera so that we know how to overlay the virtual object.

- **Camera-to-image**: This refers to the calibration parameters of the camera. This defines how we can project a 3D object onto a 2D image plane. This is the image that we will actually see in the end.

Consider the following image:

As we can see here, the car is trying to fit into the scene but it looks very artificial. If we don't convert the coordinates in the right way, it looks unnatural. This is what we were talking about in the object-to-scene transformation! Once we transform the 3D coordinates of the virtual object into the coordinate frame of the real world, we need to estimate the pose of the camera:

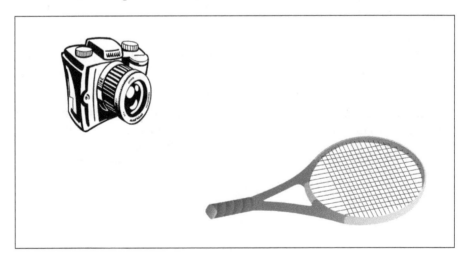

We need to understand the position and rotation of the camera because that's what the user will see. Once we estimate the camera pose, we are ready to put this 3D scene on a 2D image.

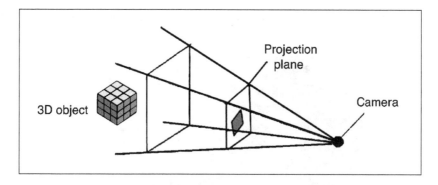

Once we have these transformations, we can build the complete system.

# What is pose estimation?

Before we proceed, we need to understand how to estimate the camera pose. This is a very critical step in an augmented reality system and we need to get it right if we want our experience to be seamless. In the world of augmented reality, we overlay graphics on top of an object in real time. In order to do that, we need to know the location and orientation of the camera, and we need to do it quickly. This is where pose estimation becomes very important. If you don't track the pose correctly, the overlaid graphics will not look natural.

Consider the following image:

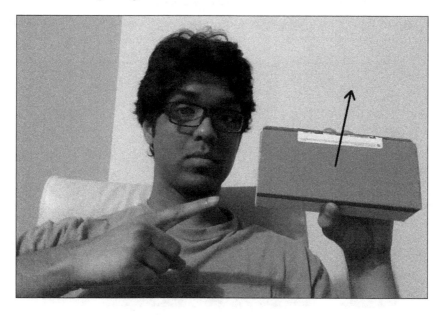

The arrow line represents that the surface is normal. Let's say the object changes its orientation:

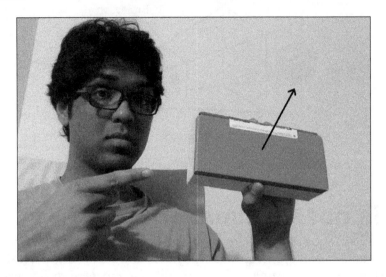

Now even though the location is the same, the orientation has changed. We need to have this information so that the overlaid graphics looks natural. We need to make sure that it's aligned to this orientation as well as position.

# How to track planar objects?

Now that you understand what pose estimation is, let's see how you can use it to track planar objects. Let's consider the following planar object:

Now if we extract feature points from this image, we will see something like this:

Let's tilt the cardboard:

As we can see, the cardboard is tilted in this image. Now if we want to make sure our virtual object is overlaid on top of this surface, we need to gather this planar tilt information. One way to do this is by using the relative positions of those feature points. If we extract the feature points from the preceding image, it will look like this:

As you can see, the feature points got closer horizontally on the far end of the plane as compared to the ones on the near end.

So we can utilize this information to extract the orientation information from the image. If you remember, we discussed perspective transformation in detail when we were discussing geometric transformations as well as panoramic imaging. All we need to do is use those two sets of points and extract the homography matrix. This homography matrix will tell us how the cardboard turned.

Consider the following image:

We start by selecting the region of interest.

We then extract feature points from this region of interest. Since we are tracking planar objects, the algorithm assumes that this region of interest is a plane. That was obvious, but it's better to state it explicitly! So make sure you have a cardboard in your hand when you select this region of interest. Also, it'll be better if the cardboard has a bunch of patterns and distinctive points so that it's easy to detect and track the feature points on it.

Let the tracking begin! We'll move the cardboard around to see what happens:

As you can see, the feature points are being tracked inside the region of interest. Let's tilt it and see what happens:

Looks like the feature points are being tracked properly. As we can see, the overlaid rectangle is changing its orientation according to the surface of the cardboard.

Here is the code to do it:

```python
import sys
from collections import namedtuple

import cv2
import numpy as np

class PoseEstimator(object):
    def __init__(self):
        # Use locality sensitive hashing algorithm
        flann_params = dict(algorithm = 6, table_number = 6,
                key_size = 12, multi_probe_level = 1)

        self.min_matches = 10
        self.cur_target = namedtuple('Current', 'image, rect,
        keypoints, descriptors, data')
        self.tracked_target = namedtuple('Tracked', 'target,
        points_prev, points_cur, H, quad')

        self.feature_detector = cv2.ORB(nfeatures=1000)
        self.feature_matcher = cv2.FlannBasedMatcher(flann_params,
{})
        self.tracking_targets = []

    # Function to add a new target for tracking
    def add_target(self, image, rect, data=None):
        x_start, y_start, x_end, y_end = rect
        keypoints, descriptors = [], []
        for keypoint, descriptor in zip(*self.detect_features(image)):
            x, y = keypoint.pt
            if x_start <= x <= x_end and y_start <= y <= y_end:
                keypoints.append(keypoint)
                descriptors.append(descriptor)

        descriptors = np.array(descriptors, dtype='uint8')
        self.feature_matcher.add([descriptors])
        target = self.cur_target(image=image, rect=rect,
        keypoints=keypoints,
                    descriptors=descriptors, data=None)
        self.tracking_targets.append(target)
```

```
# To get a list of detected objects
def track_target(self, frame):
    self.cur_keypoints, self.cur_descriptors =
    self.detect_features(frame)
    if len(self.cur_keypoints) < self.min_matches:
        return []

    matches =
    self.feature_matcher.knnMatch(self.cur_descriptors, k=2)
    matches = [match[0] for match in matches if len(match) ==
    2 and
                match[0].distance < match[1].distance * 0.75]
    if len(matches) < self.min_matches:
        return []

    matches_using_index = [[] for _ in
    xrange(len(self.tracking_targets))]
    for match in matches:
        matches_using_index[match.imgIdx].append(match)

    tracked = []
    for image_index, matches in
    enumerate(matches_using_index):
        if len(matches) < self.min_matches:
            continue

        target = self.tracking_targets[image_index]
        points_prev = [target.keypoints[m.trainIdx].pt for m
        in matches]
        points_cur = [self.cur_keypoints[m.queryIdx].pt for m
        in matches]
        points_prev, points_cur = np.float32((points_prev,
        points_cur))
        H, status = cv2.findHomography(points_prev,
        points_cur, cv2.RANSAC, 3.0)
        status = status.ravel() != 0
        if status.sum() < self.min_matches:
            continue

        points_prev, points_cur = points_prev[status],
        points_cur[status]

        x_start, y_start, x_end, y_end = target.rect
        quad = np.float32([[x_start, y_start], [x_end,
        y_start], [x_end, y_end], [x_start, y_end]])
```

```
        quad = cv2.perspectiveTransform(quad.reshape(1, -1,
        2), H).reshape(-1, 2)

        track = self.tracked_target(target=target,
        points_prev=points_prev,
                    points_cur=points_cur, H=H, quad=quad)
        tracked.append(track)

    tracked.sort(key = lambda x: len(x.points_prev),
    reverse=True)
    return tracked

# Detect features in the selected ROIs and return the keypoints
and descriptors
def detect_features(self, frame):
    keypoints, descriptors = self.feature_detector.
detectAndCompute(frame, None)
    if descriptors is None:
        descriptors = []

    return keypoints, descriptors

# Function to clear all the existing targets
def clear_targets(self):
    self.feature_matcher.clear()
    self.tracking_targets = []

class VideoHandler(object):
    def __init__(self):
        self.cap = cv2.VideoCapture(0)
        self.paused = False
        self.frame = None
        self.pose_tracker = PoseEstimator()

        cv2.namedWindow('Tracker')
        self.roi_selector = ROISelector('Tracker', self.on_rect)

    def on_rect(self, rect):
        self.pose_tracker.add_target(self.frame, rect)

    def start(self):
        while True:
            is_running = not self.paused and self.roi_selector.
selected_rect is None
```

```python
            if is_running or self.frame is None:
                ret, frame = self.cap.read()
                scaling_factor = 0.5
                frame = cv2.resize(frame, None, fx=scaling_factor,
                fy=scaling_factor,
                        interpolation=cv2.INTER_AREA)
                if not ret:
                    break

                self.frame = frame.copy()

            img = self.frame.copy()
            if is_running:
                tracked =
                self.pose_tracker.track_target(self.frame)
                for item in tracked:
                    cv2.polylines(img, [np.int32(item.quad)],
                    True, (255, 255, 255), 2)
                    for (x, y) in np.int32(item.points_cur):
                        cv2.circle(img, (x, y), 2, (255, 255,
                        255))

            self.roi_selector.draw_rect(img)
            cv2.imshow('Tracker', img)
            ch = cv2.waitKey(1)
            if ch == ord(' '):
                self.paused = not self.paused
            if ch == ord('c'):
                self.pose_tracker.clear_targets()
            if ch == 27:
                break

class ROISelector(object):
    def __init__(self, win_name, callback_func):
        self.win_name = win_name
        self.callback_func = callback_func
        cv2.setMouseCallback(self.win_name, self.on_mouse_event)
        self.selection_start = None
        self.selected_rect = None

    def on_mouse_event(self, event, x, y, flags, param):
        if event == cv2.EVENT_LBUTTONDOWN:
            self.selection_start = (x, y)
```

```
        if self.selection_start:
            if flags & cv2.EVENT_FLAG_LBUTTON:
                x_orig, y_orig = self.selection_start
                x_start, y_start = np.minimum([x_orig, y_orig],
                [x, y])
                x_end, y_end = np.maximum([x_orig, y_orig], [x,
                y])
                self.selected_rect = None
                if x_end > x_start and y_end > y_start:
                    self.selected_rect = (x_start, y_start, x_end,
                    y_end)
            else:
                rect = self.selected_rect
                self.selection_start = None
                self.selected_rect = None
                if rect:
                    self.callback_func(rect)

    def draw_rect(self, img):
        if not self.selected_rect:
            return False

        x_start, y_start, x_end, y_end = self.selected_rect
        cv2.rectangle(img, (x_start, y_start), (x_end, y_end), (0,
        255, 0), 2)
        return True

if __name__ == '__main__':
    VideoHandler().start()
```

# What happened inside the code?

To start with, we have a PoseEstimator class that does all the heavy lifting here. We need something to detect the features in the image and something to match the features between successive images. So we use the ORB feature detector and the Flann feature matcher. As we can see, we initialize the class with these parameters in the constructor.

Whenever we select a region of interest, we call the add_target method to add that to our list of tracking targets. This method just extracts the features from that region of interest and stores in one of the class variables. Now that we have a target, we are ready to track it!

The `track_target` method handles all the tracking. We take the current frame and extract all the keypoints. However, we are not really interested in all the keypoints in the current frame of the video. We just want the keypoints that belong to our target object. So now, our job is to find the closest keypoints in the current frame.

We now have a set of keypoints in the current frame and we have another set of keypoints from our target object in the previous frame. The next step is to extract the homography matrix from these matching points. This homography matrix tells us how to transform the overlaid rectangle so that it's aligned with the cardboard surface. We just need to take this homography matrix and apply it to the overlaid rectangle to obtain the new positions of all its points.

# How to augment our reality?

Now that we know how to track planar objects, let's see how to overlay 3D objects on top of the real world. The objects are 3D but the video on our screen is 2D. So the first step here is to understand how to map those 3D objects to 2D surfaces so that it looks realistic. We just need to project those 3D points onto planar surfaces.

# Mapping coordinates from 3D to 2D

Once we estimate the pose, we project the points from the 3D to the 2D. Consider the following image:

As we can see here, the TV remote control is a 3D object but we are seeing it on a 2D plane. Now if we move it around, it will look like this:

This 3D object is still on a 2D plane. The object has moved to a different location and the distance from the camera has changed as well. How do we compute these coordinates? We need a mechanism to map this 3D object onto the 2D surface. This is where the 3D to 2D projection becomes really important.

We just need to estimate the initial camera pose to start with. Now, let's assume that the intrinsic parameters of the camera are already known. So we can just use the `solvePnP` function in OpenCV to estimate the camera's pose. This function is used to estimate the object's pose using a set of points. You can read more about it at http://docs.opencv.org/modules/calib3d/doc/camera_ calibration_and_3d_reconstruction.html#bool solvePnP(InputArray objectPoints, InputArray imagePoints, InputArray cameraMatrix, InputArray distCoeffs, OutputArray rvec, OutputArray tvec, bool useExtrinsicGuess, int flags) Once we do this, we need to project these points onto 2D. We use the OpenCV function `projectPoints` to do this. This function calculates the projections of those 3D points onto the 2D plane.

# How to overlay 3D objects on a video?

Now that we have all the different blocks, we are ready to build the final system. Let's say we want to overlay a pyramid on top of our cardboard as shown here:

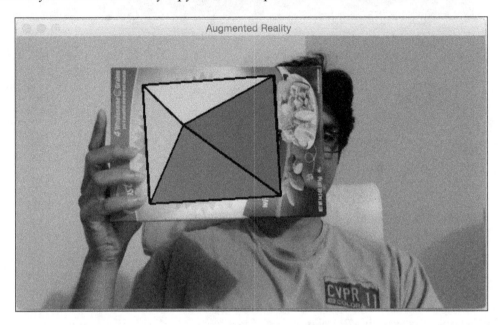

Let's tilt the cardboard to see what happens:

Looks like the pyramid is following the surface. Let's add a second target:

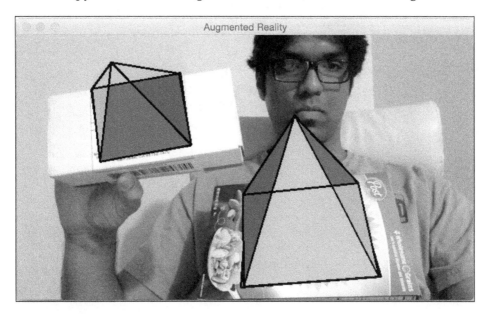

You can keep adding more targets and all those pyramids will be tracked nicely. Let's see how to do this using OpenCV Python. Make sure to save the previous file as pose_estimation.py because we will be importing a couple of classes from there:

```python
import cv2
import numpy as np

from pose_estimation import PoseEstimator, ROISelector

class Tracker(object):
    def __init__(self):
        self.cap = cv2.VideoCapture(0)
        self.frame = None
        self.paused = False
        self.tracker = PoseEstimator()

        cv2.namedWindow('Augmented Reality')
        self.roi_selector = ROISelector('Augmented Reality',
        self.on_rect)

        self.overlay_vertices = np.float32([[0, 0, 0], [0, 1, 0],
        [1, 1, 0], [1, 0, 0],
                                  [0.5, 0.5, 4]])
```

```python
        self.overlay_edges = [(0, 1), (1, 2), (2, 3), (3, 0),
                    (0,4), (1,4), (2,4), (3,4)]
        self.color_base = (0, 255, 0)
        self.color_lines = (0, 0, 0)

    def on_rect(self, rect):
        self.tracker.add_target(self.frame, rect)


    def start(self):
        while True:
            is_running = not self.paused and self.roi_selector.
selected_rect is None
            if is_running or self.frame is None:
                ret, frame = self.cap.read()
                scaling_factor = 0.5
                frame = cv2.resize(frame, None, fx=scaling_factor,
                fy=scaling_factor,
                        interpolation=cv2.INTER_AREA)
                if not ret:
                    break

                self.frame = frame.copy()

            img = self.frame.copy()
            if is_running:
                tracked = self.tracker.track_target(self.frame)
                for item in tracked:
                    cv2.polylines(img, [np.int32(item.quad)],
                    True, self.color_lines, 2)
                    for (x, y) in np.int32(item.points_cur):
                        cv2.circle(img, (x, y), 2,
                        self.color_lines)

                    self.overlay_graphics(img, item)

            self.roi_selector.draw_rect(img)
            cv2.imshow('Augmented Reality', img)
            ch = cv2.waitKey(1)
            if ch == ord(' '):
                self.paused = not self.paused
            if ch == ord('c'):
                self.tracker.clear_targets()
            if ch == 27:
                break
```

```
def overlay_graphics(self, img, tracked):
    x_start, y_start, x_end, y_end = tracked.target.rect
    quad_3d = np.float32([[x_start, y_start, 0], [x_end,
    y_start, 0],
                [x_end, y_end, 0], [x_start, y_end, 0]])
    h, w = img.shape[:2]
    K = np.float64([[w, 0, 0.5*(w-1)],
                    [0, w, 0.5*(h-1)],
                    [0, 0, 1.0]])
    dist_coef = np.zeros(4)
    ret, rvec, tvec = cv2.solvePnP(quad_3d, tracked.quad, K,
    dist_coef)
    verts = self.overlay_vertices * [(x_end-x_start),
    (y_end-y_start),
                -(x_end-x_start)*0.3] + (x_start, y_start, 0)
    verts = cv2.projectPoints(verts, rvec, tvec, K,
    dist_coef)[0].reshape(-1, 2)

    verts_floor = np.int32(verts).reshape(-1,2)
    cv2.drawContours(img, [verts_floor[:4]], -1,
    self.color_base, -3)
    cv2.drawContours(img, [np.vstack((verts_floor[:2],
    verts_floor[4:5]))],
                -1, (0,255,0), -3)
    cv2.drawContours(img, [np.vstack((verts_floor[1:3],
    verts_floor[4:5]))],
                -1, (255,0,0), -3)
    cv2.drawContours(img, [np.vstack((verts_floor[2:4],
    verts_floor[4:5]))],
                -1, (0,0,150), -3)
    cv2.drawContours(img, [np.vstack((verts_floor[3:4],
    verts_floor[0:1],
                verts_floor[4:5]))], -1, (255,255,0), -3)

    for i, j in self.overlay_edges:
        (x_start, y_start), (x_end, y_end) = verts[i],
        verts[j]
        cv2.line(img, (int(x_start), int(y_start)),
        (int(x_end), int(y_end)), self.color_lines, 2)

if __name__ == '__main__':
    Tracker().start()
```

# Let's look at the code

The class `Tracker` is used to perform all the computations here. We initialize the class with the pyramid structure that is defined using edges and vertices. The logic that we use to track the surface is the same as we discussed earlier because we are using the same class. We just need to use `solvePnP` and `projectPoints` to map the 3D pyramid to the 2D surface.

# Let's add some movements

Now that we know how to add a virtual pyramid, let's see if we can add some movements. Let's see how we can dynamically change the height of the pyramid. When you start, the pyramid will look like this:

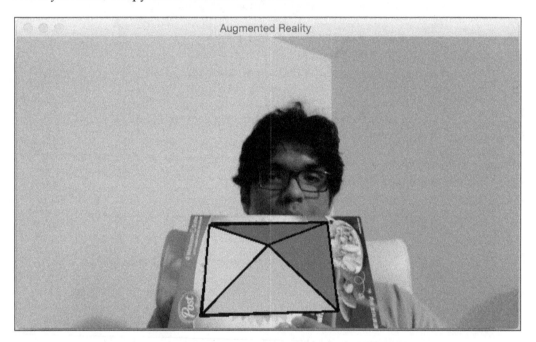

If you wait for some time, the pyramid gets taller and it will look like this:

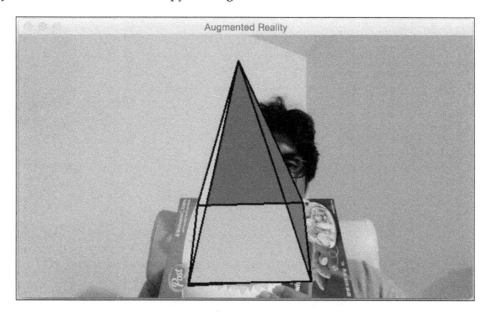

Let's see how to do it in OpenCV Python. Inside the augmented reality code that we just discussed, add the following snippet at the end of the __init__ method in the `Tracker` class:

```
self.overlay_vertices = np.float32([[0, 0, 0], [0, 1, 0], [1, 1, 0],
[1, 0, 0], [0.5, 0.5, 4]])
self.overlay_edges = [(0, 1), (1, 2), (2, 3), (3, 0),
            (0,4), (1,4), (2,4), (3,4)]
self.color_base = (0, 255, 0)
self.color_lines = (0, 0, 0)

self.graphics_counter = 0
self.time_counter = 0
```

Now that we have the structure, we need to add the code to dynamically change the height. Replace the `overlay_graphics()` method with the following method:

```
def overlay_graphics(self, img, tracked):
    x_start, y_start, x_end, y_end = tracked.target.rect
    quad_3d = np.float32([[x_start, y_start, 0],
    [x_end, y_start, 0],
```

```
                    [x_end, y_end, 0], [x_start, y_end, 0]])
h, w = img.shape[:2]
K = np.float64([[w, 0, 0.5*(w-1)],
                [0, w, 0.5*(h-1)],
                [0, 0, 1.0]])
dist_coef = np.zeros(4)
ret, rvec, tvec = cv2.solvePnP(quad_3d, tracked.quad, K,
dist_coef)


self.time_counter += 1
if not self.time_counter % 20:
    self.graphics_counter = (self.graphics_counter + 1) % 8


self.overlay_vertices = np.float32([[0, 0, 0], [0, 1, 0],
[1, 1, 0], [1, 0, 0],
                    [0.5, 0.5, self.graphics_counter]])


verts = self.overlay_vertices * [(x_end-x_start),
(y_end-y_start),
            -(x_end-x_start)*0.3] + (x_start, y_start, 0)
verts = cv2.projectPoints(verts, rvec, tvec, K,
dist_coef)[0].reshape(-1, 2)


verts_floor = np.int32(verts).reshape(-1,2)
cv2.drawContours(img, [verts_floor[:4]], -1,
self.color_base, -3)
cv2.drawContours(img, [np.vstack((verts_floor[:2],
verts_floor[4:5]))],
            -1, (0,255,0), -3)
cv2.drawContours(img, [np.vstack((verts_floor[1:3],
verts_floor[4:5]))],
            -1, (255,0,0), -3)
cv2.drawContours(img, [np.vstack((verts_floor[2:4],
verts_floor[4:5]))],
            -1, (0,0,150), -3)
cv2.drawContours(img, [np.vstack((verts_floor[3:4],
verts_floor[0:1],
            verts_floor[4:5]))], -1, (255,255,0), -3)


for i, j in self.overlay_edges:
    (x_start, y_start), (x_end, y_end) = verts[i], verts[j]
    cv2.line(img, (int(x_start), int(y_start)), (int(x_end),
    int(y_end)), self.color_lines, 2)
```

Now that we know how to change the height, let's go ahead and make the pyramid dance for us. We can make the tip of the pyramid oscillate in a nice periodic fashion. So when you start, it will look like this:

If you wait for some time, it will look like this:

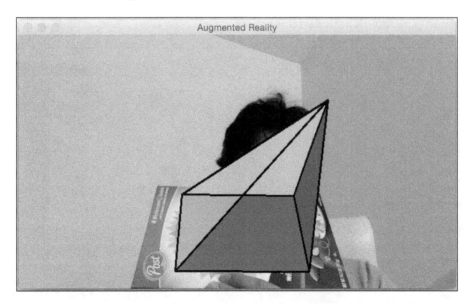

You can look at `augmented_reality_motion.py` for the implementation details.

In our next experiment, we will make the whole pyramid move around the region of interest. We can make it move in any way we want. Let's start by adding linear diagonal movement around our selected region of interest. When you start, it will look like this:

After some time, it will look like this:

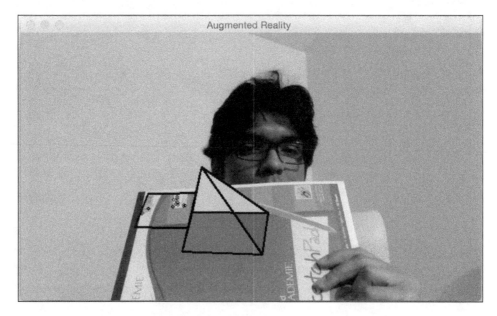

Refer to `augmented_reality_dancing.py` to see how to change the `overlay_graphics()` method to make it dance. Let's see if we can make the pyramid go around in circles around our region of interest. When you start, it will look like this:

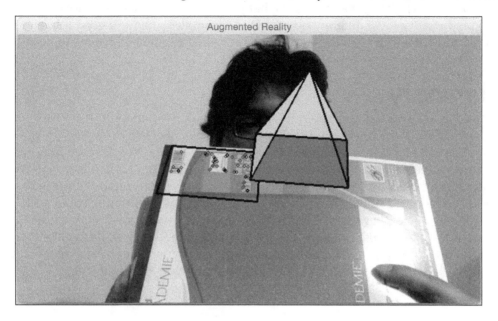

After some time, it will move to a new position:

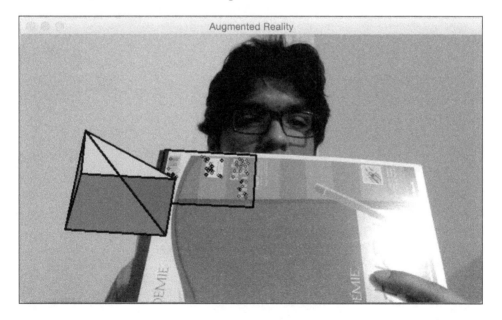

You can refer to `augmented_reality_circular_motion.py` to see how to make this happen. You can make it do anything you want. You just need to come up with the right mathematical formula and the pyramid will literally dance to your tune! You can also try out other virtual objects to see what you can with it. There are a lot of things you can do with a lot of different objects. These examples provide a good reference point, on top of which you can build many interesting augmented reality applications.

# Summary

In this chapter, you learned about the premise of augmented reality and understood what an augmented reality system looks like. We discussed the geometric transformations required for augmented reality. You learned how to use those transformations to estimate the camera pose. You learned how to track planar objects. We discussed how we can add virtual objects on top of the real world. You learned how to modify the virtual objects in different ways to add cool effects. Remember that the world of computer vision is filled with endless possibilities! This book is designed to teach you the necessary skills to get started on a wide variety of projects. Now it's up to you and your imagination to use the skills you have acquired here to build something unique and interesting.

# Index

# E

ears
  detecting 82, 83
edge detection
  about 36
  process 36-39
embossing filter 43, 44
epipolar geometry 222-230
epipolar lines
  about 223
  versus SIFT 230
epipole 223
erosion
  about 45
  using 46
eyes
  detecting 77-79
  sunglasses, positioning 80-82

# F

faces
  detecting 72, 73
  funny masks, overlaying on 74-77
  tracking 72, 73
feature based tracking 178-180
Features from Accelerated Segment
    Test (FAST) 104, 105
feature tracker
  building 178
Flann
  URL 121
frame differencing
  using 167-169
fundamental matrix 223
funny masks
  overlaying, on top of faces 74-77

# G

Gaussian Mixture Markov Random
    Field (GMMRF)
  about 163
  URL 163

geometric transformations, for augmented
    reality
  about 241
  camera-to-image 241
  object-to-scene 241
  scene-to-camera 241
GrabCut
  about 159
  reference link 159
graph-cuts 159

# H

Haar cascades
  used, for detecting things 69, 70
Hamming distance
  URL 114
Harris Corner Detector 96
Histogram Equalization 49
Homebrew 2
homography 25
HSV color space 8

# I

image color spaces 7
image content analysis 91
image filter 32
image rotation 16-18
images
  cartoonizing 60-62
  code, deconstructing 63-68
  color images, handling 50, 51
  contrast, enhancing 49, 50
  displaying 5
  expanding 133-136
  loading 6, 7
  reading 5
  saving 5-7
  stitching 121
  stretched image, reason 124
image scaling 19-21
image segmentation
  about 159-161
  working 163

# W

**watershed algorithm**
  about 163, 164
  reference link 163
**webcam**
  accessing 53, 54
  VideoCapture function, using 54
**Windows**
  OpenCV-Python, installing on 1, 2

# Y

**YUV color space 8**

**Thank you for buying**
# OpenCV with Python By Example

## About Packt Publishing

Packt, pronounced 'packed', published its first book, *Mastering phpMyAdmin for Effective MySQL Management*, in April 2004, and subsequently continued to specialize in publishing highly focused books on specific technologies and solutions.

Our books and publications share the experiences of your fellow IT professionals in adapting and customizing today's systems, applications, and frameworks. Our solution-based books give you the knowledge and power to customize the software and technologies you're using to get the job done. Packt books are more specific and less general than the IT books you have seen in the past. Our unique business model allows us to bring you more focused information, giving you more of what you need to know, and less of what you don't.

Packt is a modern yet unique publishing company that focuses on producing quality, cutting-edge books for communities of developers, administrators, and newbies alike. For more information, please visit our website at www.packtpub.com.

## About Packt Open Source

In 2010, Packt launched two new brands, Packt Open Source and Packt Enterprise, in order to continue its focus on specialization. This book is part of the Packt Open Source brand, home to books published on software built around open source licenses, and offering information to anybody from advanced developers to budding web designers. The Open Source brand also runs Packt's Open Source Royalty Scheme, by which Packt gives a royalty to each open source project about whose software a book is sold.

## Writing for Packt

We welcome all inquiries from people who are interested in authoring. Book proposals should be sent to author@packtpub.com. If your book idea is still at an early stage and you would like to discuss it first before writing a formal book proposal, then please contact us; one of our commissioning editors will get in touch with you.

We're not just looking for published authors; if you have strong technical skills but no writing experience, our experienced editors can help you develop a writing career, or simply get some additional reward for your expertise.

## OpenCV Computer Vision with Python

ISBN: 978-1-78216-392-3          Paperback: 122 pages

Learn to capture videos, manipulate images, and track objects with Python using the OpenCV Library

1. Set up OpenCV, its Python bindings, and optional Kinect drivers on Windows, Mac or Ubuntu.

2. Create an application that tracks and manipulates faces.

3. Identify face regions using normal color images and depth images.

## OpenCV Computer Vision Application Programming Cookbook
### Second Edition

ISBN: 978-1-78216-148-6          Paperback: 374 pages

Over 50 recipes to help you build computer vision applications in C++ using the OpenCV library

1. Master OpenCV, the open source library of the computer vision community.

2. Master fundamental concepts in computer vision and image processing.

3. Learn the important classes and functions of OpenCV with complete working examples applied on real images.

CPSIA information can be obtained
at www.ICGtesting.com
Printed in the USA
BVHW08s0716150918
527610BV00003B/18/P

9 781785 283932